# Sacred Bonds

Published by Awakened Media
www.awakenedmagazine.com
www.awakened.lifestyle

ISBN: 978-1-935798-29-3

Publisher / Curator: David Trotter
Cover design: Andrew O. Malbas
Interior design and layout: Julia Burtseva
Editor: Tracey Regan

For permissions or bulk orders, contact: hello@awakenedmagazine.com

*To mothers and their children,
whose relationships have been both beautiful and complicated,
may these stories remind you
that love can take many forms
and healing is always possible.*

# awakened
## magazine

**Awakened Magazine** is a leading resource for soulful storytelling, conscious living, and transformative wisdom from today's most inspiring healers, coaches, and spiritual leaders.

Subscribe for free:
www.awakenedmagazine.com

**Awakened Lifestyle** is your go-to directory to discover conscious events, healers, and podcast opportunities – locally and globally.

Explore listings or add your own:
www.awakened.lifestyle

**Awakened Hearts** is a series of heart-opening anthology books featuring real stories of spiritual awakening, healing, and transformation.

Share your story:
www.awakenedheartsbook.com

*We're here to support you on your awakening journey!*

# **Section I:** The Love That Shapes Us



# **Section II:** Becoming a Mother

# Section III: When the Bond Breaks



# Section IV: Healing, Forgiveness & Legacy

There's something about the relationship between a mother and a child that stays with us. It weaves itself into our lives, shaping how we love, grow, and connect.

Some of us were raised in homes filled with warmth, presence, and steady love. Others experienced distance, confusion, or challenge. And many of us carry a mix of both… moments of deep connection alongside moments that invited us to grow.

That's what this book holds.

When I created the *Awakened Hearts* anthology series, it was born out of a simple desire… to give people a space to share their stories in a way that helps others feel seen, understood, and less alone.

With *Sacred Bonds*, we turn toward one of the most meaningful relationships of our lives.

Inside these pages, you'll find stories of love, growth, resilience, forgiveness, and everything in between. Stories of mothers doing the best they could. Stories of children learning, evolving, and becoming.

My hope is that as you read, you'll find pieces of yourself in these stories.

Wherever this book meets you, trust that.

Because these stories aren't here to tell you what to think or how to feel. They're here to open something, to soften something, and to remind you that your story matters too.

And if something in these pages speaks to you, trust that it's meant for you… and that something within you is awakening to Love.

**David Trotter**
Curator / Publisher – *Awakened Hearts*
Co-founder / Publisher – *Awakened Magazine*

*P.S. If a particular story speaks to you, I encourage you to reach out to the author. Let them know the impact they made, or explore how they might support you on your own journey.*

# Section I:
# The Love That Shapes Us

- What did love feel like in my earliest memories?

- How did my mother express care, presence, or protection?

- In what ways did that love shape who I am today?

LONG BEFORE WE DEFINE LOVE,
IT IS ALREADY DEFINING US.

# 01

# Lily and the Rainbow: Lessons of Love, Presence, and Wonder

*by Livia Devi*

Before I ever opened my eyes, I knew her, though I did not yet understand who she was. I felt her in the rhythm of her breath, in the subtle shift of air when she was near, in a warmth that reached inside me before I even existed. When I finally arrived, screaming and startled by the sudden brightness of life, her tears fell onto my face: warm, salty, alive. They did not frighten me. They baptized me. Even then, I knew something that would anchor me for the rest of my life: I am safe. I am wanted. I belong. That knowing stayed, a quiet truth that would carry me through moments of fear, doubt, and uncertainty later in life. Perhaps that was the first lesson my mother offered without words: belonging begins in presence, not perfection, and love is the foundation on which all else grows.

As a child, I learned the value of anticipation and patience through long, quiet evenings when I would delay sleep as long as possible, negotiating for one more story, and then another, and then another, until the moon hung low and the house smelled of tangerines and firewood. Not the stories written in books, but those conjured from her imagination, memory, and spirit. I would lie still, my small body tense with expectation, listening as her voice softened, deepened, and shifted, becoming something ancient, playful, fierce, and tender all at once.

Each story was a portal into worlds where limits dissolved, where courage and curiosity were one, and where love always mattered. Even then, I sensed something profound: imagination was not escape, it was a method for understanding life, a way of practicing presence, empathy, and possibility. Those nights taught me that curiosity and creativity are as vital to life as breathing, and that those who honor them can find freedom and resilience in any circumstance. I learned, without words, that paying attention transforms reality, that to notice deeply is to participate fully in life itself.

Our home in Romania was modest, filled with furniture that had already lived many lives, walls carrying the faint imprint of every laughter, every argument, every whispered secret. If you stepped inside, you might not have noticed anything extraordinary at first, but linger long enough, and you would feel it: warmth, safety, the invisible wealth of being deeply loved.

Scarcity never touched us, because love filled every corner. Perhaps that is a truth worth carrying: material abundance is not the measure of richness, love is. I began to understand that richness is measured not by what we hold, but by how deeply we are held, by the constancy of a presence that never wavers.

I remember mornings when my mother braided my long blonde hair, her fingers moving with care, tugging gently at knots, apologizing with a soft kiss. I leaned into her chest, breathing in her familiar perfume, a scent that still lives in my nervous system decades later. "Sit straight," she would say, glancing at the clock. "I am," I would protest. "Straighter than that," she'd correct gently, teaching me that tenderness does not preclude firmness, that discipline can be an act of love, and that guidance given with care can feel like wings rather than chains.

In those moments, I learned a subtle but crucial truth: the most powerful lessons are often embedded in ordinary gestures, and love and rigor are not mutually exclusive; they are complementary. The smallest acts, done with awareness, can carry the deepest wisdom, shaping the way we move through the world long after the hands that taught us are gone.

Every afternoon, I would wait for the sound of her footsteps. The rhythm was so familiar that my body would light up even before my mind realized she had arrived. She would cross the threshold wearing flowing skirts, carrying the weight of the world with elegance. The moment she entered, everything softened. She brought safety, a quiet sanctuary, a place where life slowed and I could breathe. In her presence, I began to understand an essential truth: some people exist in the world to remind us that home is not a place, but a presence. And that presence, when sustained with love and intention, becomes a guide through every storm life offers.

Evenings were rituals of wonder. My father would spread a map of the sky across our small coffee table, pointing out constellations, galaxies, distances too vast to comprehend. The stove crackled nearby, filling the room with warmth, and the scent of tangerine peel drifted through the air, tangy and sweet. I would drift to sleep suspended between fire and cosmos, grounded and expansive, all at once. Those evenings taught me the art of balance: holding presence while imagining possibilities, being rooted while reaching outward, and learning that wisdom can come not from instruction but from living, breathing experiences of awe.

From this, I understood that even in ordinary routines, there is extraordinary potential if attention is applied with care and intention. Beauty and learning exist not just in achievement but in immersion, in the act of fully inhabiting each moment, no matter how small.

As the youngest, I often hid beneath her skirts when the world felt too big, pressing my face into her legs, shrinking into safety. She never rushed me out, never told me to be brave before I could be, and through that quiet allowance, I understood that growth requires patience, that love sometimes speaks in silence, and that strength is not always visible; it can be the gentle permission to exist fully at your own pace. From this, I realized that nurturing presence often outweighs action, and that the courage to simply be oneself is the foundation for every other form of courage.

School, however, was another universe entirely. Letters felt meaningless compared to the violin, and I refused learning the alphabet, failing first grade. Following my passion came first, ahead of conventional education, which, in my opinion, can limit the capacity of authentic expression. My parents worried, whispering about whether something was "wrong" with me, and I felt their concern even when unspoken. From an early age, I learned the tension between the world's expectations and one's own inner rhythm; the first lesson was that life often asks us to navigate spaces we do not yet understand. I also learnt that self-worth cannot always be measured by conformity.

It was in those moments of quiet resistance that I began to understand the value of listening to my inner voice by respecting my own pace and cultivating patience.

The violin became my secret companion. I remember hours spent on the edge of the sofa, bow in hand, struggling to coax the strings into sound while my mother worked nearby. When the notes scratched or squealed, she would place her hand lightly on my shoulder and whisper, "It's okay. Let the music find you. Don't chase it, let it come." In her patient attention, I learned that mastery is patience and that dedication paired with gentleness can often yield transformation. I came to understand that love is the frame in which growth naturally occurs. That lesson has followed me my entire life: sometimes, to truly inhabit your gifts, you must stop forcing and start listening. Growth, creativity, and presence are cultivated not through pressure but through patience, gentle guidance, and trust in our own rhythm. Self-compassion, I discovered, is the lens through which learning becomes a sacred experience rather than a performance, and time, not force, is the greatest teacher.

I spoke my first word at four, pointing at a television screen showing people washing themselves in the Ganges River: "Hindi." She turned, surprised, and said, "No. This is your home now, not India." I looked into her eyes, and something clicked. Language arrived not as an obligation but as a relationship, as a bridge. I realized that belonging requires engagement and trust, not force, and that understanding the world begins with presence, not compliance. Connection requires attentiveness, not control. The willingness to notice, participate, and respond is where belonging truly grows.

Liliana (Lily), my mother, an architect, a builder of spaces and possibilities, knew that guidance was key to my growth and that I did not need "fixing." She brought me to her workplace, where women adored me, and there, with newspapers and patience, we learned the letters together. It was not just letters I learned, but how learning itself could be infused with love, and that patience and encouragement often teach more than punishment or pressure ever can. From this,

I have carried the understanding that learning, like life, flourishes when nurtured with kindness rather than coerced through fear or expectation. Attention, care, and encouragement are the unseen architecture of possibility—the scaffolding that allows a person to grow into their fullest potential without fear or judgment.

When I graduated from a special-needs class with an A, her pride lit something inside me, and I made a quiet vow: I will keep becoming, *for you.* Excellence became my love language, expressed not from obligation but devotion, a lesson in how love can transform expectation into inspiration, and how nurturing another's joy can awaken our own potential. Our relationships can shape our aspirations more profoundly than external pressures ever can; love often teaches ambition without resentment, and the insight is clear—when we act out of love, we expand not only ourselves but the hearts of those around us.

At eleven, I wrote a story about an alien spacecraft, channeling something wild and unfiltered that I did not yet understand. I handed it to her nervously. She read quietly, then looked up, her eyes shining: "Take this to your teacher. You need to share this." I won the competition, and she whispered, "You are like me. I'll tell you more when you're older." I realized then that belief can be more powerful than instruction. Encouragement can unlock hidden parts of a person's soul, and sometimes, the quiet faith of one person can carry you across oceans of self-doubt. Encouragement creates courage, and courage nurtures growth.

My adolescence was a time of quiet reflection and small rebellions. One afternoon, sitting on the balcony with her, violin across my knees, fingers sore from practice, heart heavy with self-doubt after an argument with my father about grades, I felt invisible and misunderstood. She handed me a cup of tea, the steam curling around my face, and said, "Do you hear the music?"

I shook my head.

"It's there, in every mistake, in every wrong note. You are hearing it wrong because you are trying to control it. Listen with your soul."

In that moment, I realized life, like music, often demands surrender before mastery and patience before pride. We are more than our mistakes, and letting go of control allows hidden gifts to emerge. Having a little compassion for ourselves is a prerequisite for growth. Every struggle, every failure, and every awkward step is fertile ground for transformation.

We traveled together frequently, exploring countries, cultures, and the boundless ways the world could stir our hearts. In Ireland, I remember the mist curling over the rolling green hills, the rain soft on our faces, and her laughter echoing across empty cliffs as we ran along the coast. We paused at small cafés in sleepy villages, sipping warm tea as the peat fire crackled, her hand holding mine as we watched fog drift over the fields. Even in these quiet, ordinary moments, she taught me to truly see, to notice the patterns of light on stone walls, the way the wind made the grass shimmer, the subtle joy in shared silence. Life, she showed me, is woven from these details, and attention—the willingness to be present—is the truest currency of love. The insight here is universal: being present in the moment transforms the mundane into the extraordinary.

In Paris, France, we wandered the halls of the Louvre, surrounded by centuries of art, history pressing into our awareness like an invisible heartbeat. I remember her standing beside me in front of the Mona Lisa, eyes wide with delight, a laugh slipping from my lips as I tried to mimic her fascination. "Do you see her smile?" she asked, her voice soft. "It's not the painting, it's the noticing, it's in how you allow yourself to be moved." The light caught the gilded frames, the marble floors smooth beneath our feet, and in that moment, I understood that she was teaching me how to fully inhabit wonder, how to slow down, how to feel. Later, at Disneyland, we abandoned adult expectations entirely, running through rain-spattered streets and riding on roller coasters, laughing until our stomachs ached.

All these experiences taught me that life's intensity is best experienced when shared. Joy is contagious, and shared delight expresses love through embodiment, not instruction. The lesson is simple: the deeper the shared experience, the more profound the transformation of ordinary moments into memories that sustain the heart for a lifetime.

Even simple evenings on the balcony became lessons. Tea steaming between our hands, wind whispering through the trees, birds singing, and her humming softly, I understood that intimacy is not always grand—it is presence, attention, and the willingness to witness life with care. These small rituals became my blueprint for connection with others. The depth of a relationship is measured not by grand gestures, but by the consistency of attention and care.

In April 2025, the word terminal entered our lives. Even as her body weakened, her spirit did not. One fragile evening, holding her hand, she whispered, "I'm not leaving you."

"I know," I replied, tears streaming, memorizing the warmth of her skin.

"I'll meet you over the rainbow," she said.

"I'll look for you there," I whispered back, understanding that love transcends physicality, that connection does not require proximity, and that some bonds are eternal.

She passed in July 2025, on the day she was born, completing the circle. Her ashes were later scattered in Hawaii, her favorite place on Earth, over the rainbow that stretched above the ocean waves; a final gift of freedom, joy, and color, a reminder that she had always been light and would remain so forever. In her absence, I have learned that love does not end—it transforms, becoming memory, guidance, courage, and intuition. It is always present, whispering in moments of pause, urging us toward patience and compassion.

If you are reading this and longing for your mother, know this: the bond lives in you, shaping you, teaching you, transforming you. It is not diminished by distance, time, or death. It becomes wisdom, a heartbeat, an energy you can carry into every choice, every act, every encounter.

"Mom," I whisper, in the quiet of a room that once held her laughter, "see you over the rainbow."

"Always," she answers.

And I believe her.

# Livia Devi

**Livia Devi** is at the forefront of empowering, transformative, and paradigm-breaking programs and activations for a global community of entrepreneurs, conscious creators, change-makers, thought leaders, and influencers. Co-creating her teachings with an advanced 7D collective consciousness, the Arcturian Council of Light, Livia serves as a catalyst for the New Earth, guiding individuals and organizations into a new era of technological innovation, spiritual evolution, and conscious leadership.

Through her work, Livia bridges multidimensional wisdom with practical, real-world strategies, helping visionaries embody their highest potential, expand their impact, and co-create a world rooted in unity, abundance, and enlightened consciousness. Her unique approach blends futuristic insight, energetic activation, and visionary entrepreneurship to empower the next generation of leaders and change-makers shaping the New Earth.

⊕ www.LiviaDevi.com
◎ @arcturianschanneling
Scan QR code to learn more about Livia Devi.

# 02

# The Love That Raised Me

*by Yasmin Elzomor*

My mother's love has never been loud or flashy. It's always been steady, trustworthy, and grounded. It's the kind of love that doesn't need to convince you it's real because you've never known life without it. I feel blessed to say that from my earliest memories, love wasn't something I searched for; it was something I was born into.

She had me at forty-five, an age when many women are told their time has passed. Getting pregnant took time. There was waiting, uncertainty, and plenty of moments when it probably felt like it wasn't going to happen. She would witness other friends and family members easily conceive, and it would get to her, but she wouldn't talk much about it. She just kept going to appointments, kept living her life, and didn't let the disappointment turn into resentment. She accepted what she couldn't control without giving up on what she still wanted. After several miscarriages and many years of trying and waiting, I finally arrived. She always tells me how I was born into a love that had been preparing for me for years. Both she and my dad were ecstatic. My brother, who is eight years older than I, was also excited to have me join the family.

Knowing my mom's fertility journey has shaped how I understand my own existence. I was intentional, I was chosen, and I was deeply wanted. Knowing this shaped how I move through the world. By the time I arrived, she had lived, learned, endured, healed, and softened. She had already met herself. And because of that, she met me with clarity. There was no confusion about her role, no resentment about what she had given up, no sense of loss about paths she didn't take. She didn't see me as something that took from her life; she saw me as something that completed it. As a thirty-one-year-old woman who desires to eventually have a family, this inspires me, and I hope that I will be ready when the moment arrives... if it's meant to arrive. As a woman, there's so much pressure around having children at the "right" time, and we're always worried that the biological clock is ticking away, so being able to witness my mom break these societal expectations and rules has helped me expand my possibilities.

With my mom, I never had to perform. I didn't have to become more palatable, more impressive, or more agreeable to earn affection. I felt like I was allowed to be exactly who I was. I was allowed to change and grow. I didn't have to have everything figured out. That kind of acceptance does something profound to a child. It teaches you that love isn't something you barter for, and that your worth is inherent, not conditional. It teaches you that being seen is just as important as being protected.

There were moments growing up when I didn't fully understand the weight of what she was giving me. It's only with time—and with witnessing other relationships—that I've realized how rare our dynamic truly is. Many people grow up feeling misunderstood, unseen, or pressured to become versions of themselves that earn approval. I grew up feeling trusted. Our relationship has evolved so much over the years, and I'm grateful for every moment. As I've grown older, our connection has only gotten stronger and closer. This doesn't mean we see eye to eye on everything or that we never disagree… but we respect each other's perspectives and know how to find common ground. Not only do we have fun together, but my mom and I grow spiritually together. If there's anyone who loves learning and expanding her mind more than I, it's my mother. One thing I love about my bond with her is that we recognize each other as individuals, not just roles. She is my mother, yes—but she is also a woman with her own history, strength, and personality. And she allowed me to see that. Seeing her as a whole person taught me empathy. It also taught me that I am safe to be my complete and total self with her.

I sometimes think about how different my life might have been if she'd become a mother earlier in life. If I'd been born into a different season of her life, one with less certainty, self-knowledge, or peace. And every time, I return to the same conclusion: I arrived exactly when I was meant to. Her timing was not delayed; it was absolutely divine.

I carry her influence in ways I'm still discovering. In how I respond to vulnerability. In how I treat uncertainty and how I hold compassion for others without abandoning my own needs. She didn't just raise me, she shaped my inner world. I don't take our relationship for granted. As I move through life, I understand more clearly how much of who I am traces back to how she loved me. So much of what she taught me and instilled in me from a young age lives within me.

This bond is sacred not because it's perfect, but because it was intentional. It was built with care, maintained with honor and respect, and deepened with time. My mother didn't just give me life, she taught me that love can be both gentle and powerful, and that waiting can be an act of devotion. I'm here because she believed. I'm grounded because she was steady. I'm loved because she chose me in ways both big and small. And that is a sacred bond I will carry with me for the rest of my life.

Yasmin Elzomor (right) and her Mom

# Yasmin Elzomor

**Yasmin Elzomor** is a transformational guide, thought leader, spiritual mentor, speaker, author, and podcast host of Humanity Feels. She helps people reclaim their power, embody their truth, and create freedom in love, intimacy, and life. After a profound and sudden spiritual awakening at the age of 21, and a journey through heartbreak and self-reconstruction, she emerged from rock bottom with a fierce dedication to help others alchemize pain into power and rebuild from their own destruction. With empathy, intuitive wisdom, and unwavering honesty, Yasmin guides people through deep inner work, helping them confront shadows, rewrite narratives, awaken to their sovereignty, and step into their true power. More than a mentor, she is a visionary, alchemist, truth seeker, and creative force, leading with integrity and lighting a path for others to rise into their fullest potential.

🌐 www.YasminElzomor.com
📷 @yasminelzomor
Scan QR code to learn more about Yasmin Elzomor.

25

# 03

# The Soul Knows:
# Dance Choreographed Among the Stars

*by Susan Melnikow*

"Susan… PUSH! PUSH … You can do this … HARDER … Push harder… you're almost there." My midwife kept encouraging me as I tried the hardest I could to push my baby out. My husband quietly supported me as I sat with my back against him. I felt as though my body would rip wide open if I were to push any harder. It didn't matter that I had attended dozens of births as a midwife, supporting other women through this process. I honestly had no idea of the intensity and pain that labor and birth entailed.

When labor started twelve hours earlier, the powerful strength and sensation of contractions made me question my decision to give birth at home… *what was I thinking?* No wonder mothers desired anesthesia. But I was a university-trained midwife who practiced home birth and didn't want to use any medication at all. I was resolved to do this… and was also resolved to let my midwife sleep through the night, waiting until morning to call her.

I wanted an undisturbed, "physiologic birth." As I rocked gently in my rocker… b-a-c-k and f-o-r-t-h … b-a-c-k and f-o-r-t-h… my mind thought of all the tools I used to assist others during labor. I gradually followed my own advice. I slowed my breathing, relaxed my body, one muscle at a time, and gradually felt myself move into a different state of being. I eventually achieved a truly altered state of consciousness where I no longer had the sensation of pain and felt myself outside of my body, observing my body from the ceiling.

Through the darkened hours of the night, I moved from the rocking chair to the shower and back to the rocking chair, no longer mentally assessing the process. Instead, I became aware of this very special little being inside of me, knowing I was not alone, but that we were paired and doing this together. I never worried about her, as I intuitively knew she was well. Occasionally, she would give a little kick here and there to reinforce that, but more importantly, I was very aware of her presence—that soul essence that communicated we were on this journey together and all was well.

As the morning light filtered through the curtains, I finally felt the greatest pressure of my life, and a true feeling that my bottom would explode! "Susan, feel her head… It's right here." I moved my hand down, and there was her hard, little head… right there. Just the encouragement I needed to finish the process. A couple of harder, but slow pushes with panting, and out she emerged, as my midwife and I gently lifted her up to my chest together. It was her—the most gorgeous baby in the world. The SAME beautiful baby with chestnut hair and almond eyes who had visited me in a dream fourteen years earlier.

Being a mother to my daughter has been the highlight of my life. Second, has been the honor to serve many other women on their journey into motherhood during my forty-year career as a Nurse Midwife. I have witnessed many sides of motherhood and what it means to be a mother; the incredible love, wonder, beauty, and gratification, as well as the fatigue, anguish, sacrifice, and deep responsibility that it carries. The unexplainable and most beautiful aspect of becoming my daughter's mother was the indescribable love that welled up within me as soon as I held her. She felt familiar, my heart resonated with hers, and I realized I already knew her well.

I am a private person.

Certain things we learn to hold close to our hearts; the shadows that play within the underbelly of all human beings. Those things that are not to be divulged, not to be exposed to the light, to the critical judgement of others. This is one of those untold shadow stories. It is also a soul story, a story of awakening to remembrance and the hidden realm of the workings and beauty of soul: "the dance of souls."

At the age of nineteen, I had an unplanned pregnancy. It was quite a surprise, and my partner and I agonized over what to do. We both knew we wanted to become parents at some time in the future, but not at that time in our lives. He had just started college in another state, and I was attending community college in preparation for Nursing School. As we considered all options available to us, it became apparent that "not keeping the pregnancy" seemed to be the most viable.

I knew in my heart that if I were to carry a pregnancy and give birth, I would never be able to give the baby up for adoption; I also knew we were in no position to provide for a child at that time. Roe vs Wade had just travelled through the court system, all the way to the Supreme Court, and had been decided, but not yet enacted. It would become legal in just three months.

Abortion was still a very dark shadow issue, sometimes seen as an evil act, equivalent to a murderous taking of life. I wrestled, in angst, as to what the right decision would be; my mind struggled with the possibilities of what to do. If I were to pursue that route, legally, I would first need to see a psychiatrist who would determine if the pregnancy was a threat to my mental state and overall welfare. This decision weighed heavily within my whole being, as I struggled to see what the right path was for us all. And then one night, I had a very life-like and poignant dream.

In my dream, a baby came to me. It was a beautiful girl who spoke to me in a lovingly quiet voice. She told me it was OK—all would be alright if I decided not to carry the pregnancy, and that she would come to join me at a future time. She repeatedly reassured me in a heartfelt and loving manner. I awoke that morning with a fresh image of her. I felt calmer and more relaxed; I now accepted that having an abortion would be an appropriate option. The one strange question left in my mind was that this baby's appearance was Asian, which was a puzzle to me and impossible for the current pregnancy. I wondered about it, but let it go.

I realized that the termination of this pregnancy was the kindest decision I could make… really an act of love. I knew the fetus was physiologically totally dependent upon my body and, at this early stage, would be unable to exist without me. I also intuitively knew that as human beings, we are a sacred essence: a Soul that incarnates into the body. The Soul exists within another realm until the decision is made to incarnate, with purpose, to experience what it is to be human, while in a body during life on Earth. I felt that this dream baby had released me from a sacred contract, with our love to be resumed at a later time.

During the 20th century, as knowledge and understanding of the human body evolved through science, we started to focus more and more upon physical aspects of pregnancy, forgetting or not understanding the dynamic interplay of "mind, body, and spirit." The concept of Soul, or the idea that perhaps the baby is also a participant in the birth process, was never considered. I started my nursing career in the mid-1970s. I was clearly drawn to working with babies, children, and the birthing process. At that time, I was not aware of the connection with my own abortion experience and the calling I had to this nursing work.

When I graduated, I was offered the opportunity to work in a Graduate Training Program at a Labor and Delivery Unit within a prominent hospital. I was excited and immediately accepted. I lasted three months. I could not, in good conscience, perform the duties that were expected of me as part of the job at that time. It was my responsibility to assess a laboring mother, so I could move her into the delivery room at exactly the right time.

This meant she had to be completely dilated, and either pushing or ready to push her baby out. But not too soon and not too late, or I would hear the wrath of the obstetrician. The comfort, desires, and wishes of the mother were not taken into consideration at all. Once in the delivery room, it was my responsibility to get her onto a flat stainless-steel table, with her legs spread open and her feet up in stirrups. Then I was to strap both of her wrists to the table with leather straps! The vulnerability this created for the mother was unimaginable to me. If she happened to be loud or screaming with her pain, it was more than once that I heard a doctor saying, "Shut up, you should have thought about this before you got pregnant."

It was unconscionable. It was also accepted practice to exclude fathers, or any other friends and family, from the delivery room. The mother was on her own, except for any support she might get from a compassionate nurse. My stomach was in knots for the entire three months. I vowed that when it was my time to give birth, I would fare much better at home. After that, I changed course and became a pediatric nurse, working in Pediatric Intensive Care for three years.

These practices within women's health care, and particularly birth care, were part of the impetus for the Women's Liberation Movement that took off during the 1970s. The Women's Movement helped to spawn the Homebirth Movement, as well as the advancement of mid-wifery. When I took that first nursing position in Labor & Delivery, I was totally unaware that there was such a thing as a Certified Nurse Midwife. I was called to work with pregnancy and birth, but didn't understand the intricacies of expectations surrounding my role. I didn't know that technology and fetal monitors would eventually become a leading factor of importance in care. Medical care does not consider maternal intuitive or instinctual factors. As medicine has advanced, no credence is given to anything that is seen as "non-scientific," or that cannot be materially proven "beyond a shadow of a doubt." As society has evolved in response to that, anything non-evidential, such as intuition, has been discounted and even ridiculed. I have watched as mothers have lost that instinctual, sensitive, intuitive "knowing."

Historically, there's been no evidence of the existence of Soul. Western culture has developed within the context of science and materialism. Our scientific paradigm has brought many wonderful discoveries, but has also created the concept that nothing exists if it cannot be materially seen or touched. After I gave birth to my daughter, several of my colleagues and friends asked me if I hadn't been worried about my baby before my midwife's arrival, as no one was listening to her heartbeat or externally monitoring and observing labor.

It was an interesting question for me. As a midwife, I understand the importance of having a trained and experienced attendant who is paying attention to all those observable, physical things that tell us both mom and baby are well. I would never advocate for an unattended birth, but as a laboring mother, not once did I consider those things. I was connected to my daughter in an energetic way, in which I was totally secure that she was well, within this dance we were doing together.

Many Eastern religions are built upon the concept of the importance of the Soul. There is also increasing evidence that Souls choose a life path, as well as the other Souls with whom they will share that lifetime. Soul contracts will be agreed upon prior to entering an important lifetime relationship. Several religions believe that the Soul does not enter the fetus until four to six months of pregnancy, once a Soul understanding and agreement has been established between the mother and the baby. While these ideas are not collectively acknowledged within our society, they are gaining acceptance as more evidence mounts. Many people who have sustained a Near-Death Experience (NDE) are now publicly sharing their experiences of meeting spiritual entities in the heavenly realms. There is also increased documentation of communication, through Evidential Mediums, with the Souls of people who have transitioned after death.

We are moving into a time of greater understanding of the complexities of being human. We are learning about consciousness, molecular and cellular biology, physics, energy, and the connection of all living things. Through more recent explorations, we've come to understand that unseen energy fields do exist and can impact material constructs. Throughout my nursing career, I have had the honor to experience the transition of Souls both during birth and death, and to be able to feel the energy that accompanies these transitions.

Several years ago, I was invited to attend a channeling session with a well-known Medium. The sponsor of the gathering was a physicist who had been studying energy and spirituality. There were thirty people present, including many scientists and health care providers. It was my first experience of this kind, and I was unsure of what to expect.

Soft music was played as the Medium talked us through a lovely meditation. The music ceased, and we were all in our own meditative state. Gradually, I started to hear another form of music, sounding like soft harps and beautiful voices, very faintly in the distance. I later learned this was "music of the spheres": a term first created by Pythagoras in the 6th century BC, to define music existing in the heavenly realms beyond the veil that separates our earthly existence. He theorized that it was created by the movement of planets and stars, producing a constant cosmic, harmonious sound that was not usually audible to human ears. I also smelled fragrant roses, which the Medium explained to me represented the presence of the Cosmic Mother.

The Medium approached me and spoke to me softly as I opened my eyes. "There are three souls here who want to speak to you. Your mother is here, your grandfather is here, and a very young baby is here. Do you know who that might be?" I immediately understood that it was a baby I'd recently cared for during labor.

I'd had a difficult experience a few weeks previously… and I was still reeling from it. I was caring for a laboring woman at the birth center where I worked. She had a perfectly normal pregnancy, with a normal anatomy ultrasound of the baby and the placenta. I deemed her low risk and appropriate for an "out-of-hospital" birth. Initially in labor, all checked out as expected, and she was progressing well with normal baby heart tones.

Gradually, we started to hear erratic slowing of the baby's heart beyond what was acceptable… and then a very fast acceleration of the heart. This baby was clearly in distress. We called 911, and I travelled with the mom for the five-minute ambulance ride to the hospital, continuing to check the baby's heartbeat. When we got there, the baby's heart was barely audible and extremely slow. Luckily, the mother was able to push the baby out very quickly, but he had no heartbeat at birth and required full resuscitation. He was then taken to the Neonatal Intensive Care Unit, where he remained for five days on life support, until the decision needed to be made to remove it, as he could not survive on his own. The lab later found issues with the placenta, which had not been reported on the ultrasound report.

Needless to say, this was devastating for his mother. I was also feeling traumatized. I continued to meet with her to provide necessary care and emotional support. My mind kept processing, repeatedly, as to whether or not I had missed something through the pregnancy; I reviewed all facts, tests, and ultrasound reports we had in her chart.

As the Medium spoke, I recalled this baby's birth; my body and brain felt frozen again, as the pain of the experience resurfaced. "This baby is asking for a favor from you. He says nothing was your fault. Nothing was his mother's fault. He is telling me that he had a heart defect that had not shown and wasn't diagnosed. He chose not to stay, as he did not want to live a compromised life that this condition would have created. He wants you to tell his mother this. Can you do that?" I looked at the Medium in amazement. I thought about it and then agreed to do it… and she conveyed this to the baby.

That night, I thought about the day's events and wondered, *how in the world would I communicate this to his mom without her thinking I was crazy and never trusting me again?*

I slept on it, and in the morning, a solution came to me. I would tell his mom that I'd had a dream in which her baby came to me and told me about his condition, and to reassure her, she'd done nothing wrong. I would be seeing her again at the end of the week; this seemed like the best way to approach it.

When the day of the appointment arrived, I was nervous but had resolved that this was something I must do. We met together in the office, and I shared about my "dream." She burst into tears, got up, grabbed me in a huge hug, and said, "Thank you. Thank you. Thank you. That makes me feel so much better!" She was clearly able to accept this, and it was exactly what she needed to hear at that time. The ability to help her find even a small degree of comfort was comforting for me as well. This whole experience facilitated the expansion of my consciousness with the increased ability to focus, not only on the physical needs of a pregnancy and the emotional needs of a mother, but also on the Soul needs of a baby. I have come to understand the role that they play during pregnancy, labor, and birth.

The challenge we face in today's world is how to navigate our focus with a remembrance that we are not only a physical human being, but also, we are a Sacred Soul within our body. We must learn to spend time in private, quiet focus, rather than constantly being focused externally, attached to our electronic devices and the noise of the modern world. During pregnancy, if mothers spend quiet time getting to know their baby, with conscious listening for anything that may be communicated from the baby's Soul, they will come to know their baby at the Soul level. I believe this is part of what our current world needs.

I have had the honor of attending international gatherings in Colombia with Indigenous peoples from all corners of the Earth. We were invited to bring tents and sleeping bags to stay within the land territory that is part of the Kagaba (Kogi) Nation. They reside high in the Sierra Nevada de Santa Marta Mountains, with three other tribes. Their ancestors fled the Spanish conquest in the 1500s, going to the top of those mountains, evading colonization. Surprisingly, they were able to totally avoid the colonizers, thus able to retain their original indigenous culture and ways of living. There has been no outside contact until very recently. These tribes live in a strong connection to Spirit. Their spiritual teachers, or "Mamos," provide guidance from "Aluna," the conscious sacred creative source of all.

In 2011, the Mamos received communication from Aluna that it was time to open their village to the outside world. They reached out to the Western world to provide "Original Instruction" with a purpose to "save the planet," bringing back alignment and balance. They divined a message that this was necessary for the continuance of humanity's ability to maintain life on Planet Earth.

I attended the gathering, "Dawn of a New Time," where we had ten days of instruction on the original ways, including planting and harvesting, childhood education, weaving, and animal husbandry, etc. All aspects of human life come down to what many indigenous peoples refer to as "right relationship." "Right relationship" is the concept that all things are connected as one, and that we are not separate from each other, nor any aspect of Nature. We are connected to rocks, plants, trees, water, and every living creature on the planet. They believe that all things are an aspect of creation, interdependent one upon the other. As such, we must conduct ourselves with the understanding that every action we take has an effect on all. Therefore, the way in which we act must be done in "right relationship," demonstrating mutual respect. They believe that the world was created in divine perfection, and we must learn and follow the ways and teachings that Nature exhibits.

The Mamos are in divine communication with Aluna in order to receive appropriate instruction as to "right relationship" for all aspects of life and human behavior. We learned that when a young couple desires to marry, they are given counsel by the Mamos as to the advisement of such. When a baby has been conceived, again, they advise the couple about the Soul of the baby and give guidance on the purpose of this baby's life. In this way, parents are facilitated as to how to guide each child into alignment with their Soul purpose for this lifetime.

Some of the teachings included prophecies from different tribes around the world, regarding the times we are living in. It has been referred to as "The Great Turning": the ending of a 26,000-year period that is moving into a new beginning on Planet Earth. Native Americans refer to 2025 and 2026 as "A Great Winter." The Indigenous believe that many of the changes occurring on the planet are due to a lack of harmony in the way humanity is inhabiting the Earth. This includes the modern world's overuse of the planet's resources, resulting in imbalance and devastation to Nature, as well as our lack of understanding of "right relationship" and how to live. We were taught that the "Original Teachings" are based on the importance of living life with a focus on the impact "for the next seven generations." This can be distilled down to Right Relationship, Respect, Responsibility, and Reciprocity. With an intention to these concepts, we live life in harmony with Nature for "the next seven generations," allowing for a sustainable future for all beings on Planet Earth.

I firmly believe that each Soul comes into human form with a purpose and a mission for this lifetime. Within our own culture, we often parent in a way that *negates* the child's true purpose. Rather than listening and guiding the child to find their own path, we often try to push our children into our own preconceived ideas of what we want for them. Our own expectations are formed from the external society's priorities.

As we do this, we cause chaotic confusion within our children, putting them at odds with their Soul purpose for this lifetime. As a child grows and matures, they often desire to please, wanting to meet their parents' expectations. This may lead them away from their own instinctual interests; those things for which they were born with special skills or natural attributes. On a larger scale, this creates distortion in the world.

Alternatively, if we learn to listen and provide guidance, we help our children find the truth of who they are. Then, we facilitate their ability to claim their Soul identity. I believe that if we, as parents, take responsibility to help our children grow and evolve as the Sacred Souls they are, we would be a step closer to restoring balance in the world, thereby establishing the ability to live harmoniously in peace with each other.

Life is sacred. Life is complex. It is much more than our current Western mind and understanding can comprehend. Love is the unseen energy of life force, which connects it all. My experiences illustrate the mystical sacred bond between a child and their mother. Sacred contracts and relationships exist between Souls residing in unseen realms and human beings within our planetary existence. Birth and death are the gateways: the beginnings and endings in which the Soul connects with human lifeform, where heaven meets Earth.

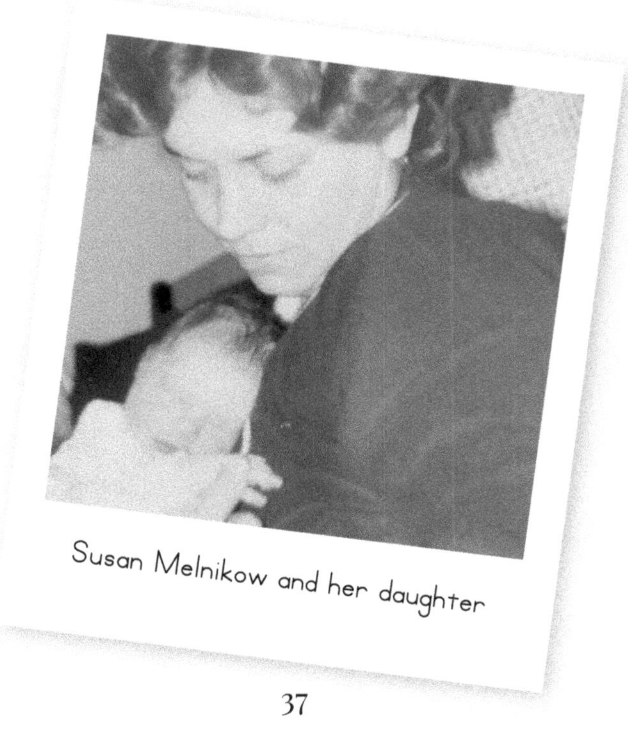

Susan Melnikow and her daughter

# Susan Melnikow

**Susan Melnikow** is an Elder Transformational Midwife. She is a mother, stepmother, and Minister of Walking Prayer, having studied with the Center for Sacred Studies, learning Earth-based ways of sacred living. She is a retired Certified Nurse Midwife with a forty-year career, caring for pregnant families and birthing babies. Susan facilitates exploration, education, and guidance through the myriads of life transitions, including pregnancy and birth, marriage, divorce, loss, and grief. Susan has extensive experience providing individual and group sessions, both virtually and in person. She is also a Ceremonialist and Celebrant, officiating at weddings, baby naming ceremonies, and celebrations of life. Susan values living in sync with Spirit and loves facilitating connections to personal Divine pathways.

www.facebook.com/susan.melnikow
Scan QR code to learn more about Susan Melnikow.

# 04

# Contracts of the Heart: Understanding Parenting from the Akashic Perspective

*by Lisa Barnett*

I had never thought much about being a mother. I did the average amount of babysitting when I was a teenager and liked little kids, but never really felt a call to be a parent. I had plenty of friends who were excited about being a mom, but that wasn't me. As a matter of fact, during my first marriage, I thought I might want to have a child, but realized I wasn't interested, at that time, with that person.

One of the fascinating gifts I've received from being able to access the Akashic Records is the ability to ask, "Why?"

*Why not with that person?* "Because your parental soul contract was not with him."

*What was that first marriage contract about?* "It was a Karmic Contract. It helped you to complete a Karmic Pattern that was important for you to understand and complete. To realize it wasn't your job to save everyone, including your husband. That learning about your karmic pattern saved you from burning yourself out as a healer."

But everything changed a few years later, after I was divorced and had completed that Karmic Contract.

I met the great "love of my life," and we bought a five-bedroom, three-bath house. I joked about all the rooms, and he said, "Don't worry, we'll fill them up." I had doubts about that, because at that point I was thinking, one cute little baby isn't going to fill up five bedrooms, but our souls had other plans.

When we decided we wanted children, I couldn't get pregnant. We ran tests, and the doctors were puzzled because the results looked fine. For three years, we had monthly disappointments. The emotional roller coaster—hormones, waiting, more bad tests; it made my heart heavy.

We eventually consulted a fertility specialist. IVF was an option, but it was costly. I was 36, so the clinic offered a decent chance, but the price was in the thousands of dollars, which we didn't have. Instead, we chose exploratory laparoscopy, covered by insurance. The surgeon found scar tissue and one damaged fallopian tube; the other tube was clear. He removed the scar tissue and said, "You should be pregnant within six months." I was.

I worked right up to my due date, then took a couple of weeks off and gave birth to our son, Connor. Going from fifteen years as a production director in advertising to being a stay-at-home mom was a big shift: changing diapers, cleaning the house, cooking, and filling hours that had been packed with work.

Before Connor turned one, I realized I was getting close to forty, and if we wanted another child, we should start trying. I worried another pregnancy might take years. Though since the "plumbing" was fixed, we conceived on the first try. We were on vacation in the Caribbean. I had checked my calendar and knew I would ovulate during the full moon that fell on Mother's Day. I knew that would be the auspicious day to get pregnant, but I didn't know how auspicious it was until a few months later.

When I realized I was pregnant, I made that next doctor's appointment to get things rolling. I was thirty-nine years old, and the doctors wanted to do some ultrasounds. Of course, as you get older, the risks are greater. I clearly remember going to the doctor's office for that ultrasound. I was about three months pregnant and had only gained one pound. I thought, *this is going to be a tiny little girl.* As I lay on that table looking at the ultrasound screen, I saw a little baby. And then the nurse moved the wand. It looked like the baby flipped over, then flipped back, then flipped over, then flipped back. As I stared in confusion, I said, "Why is that happening? What is going on with the baby?" She replied, "You have twins." I was so shocked that I immediately started crying. Connor was just one, and the thought of having newborn twins in a few months was overwhelming. Motherhood didn't feel like it came easily to me. It felt like I had to learn how to be a mom.

I joined the local Mothers' Club when Connor was a few months old, so I could meet other mothers. I needed friends, someone to have playdates and coffee with. I was hoping to learn how to 'mother' from them. At almost forty, I had spent most of my life in the corporate advertising world and felt that a natural maternal instinct was missing.

One mother in the group had twin boys, and I would watch her manage them, thinking *How do you juggle two?* My soul, however, liked a challenge. Turning forty with a one-and-a-half-year-old and newborn twins was exactly the kind of learning my soul sought.

Around the same time, my fourteen-year-old nephew moved in because his mother had gone to rehab. We lived close by, so he could stay in his school. Almost overnight, we went from one quiet "Buddha" baby to newborn twins, a toddler, and a teenager. I remember crying when the twins cried; exhaustion and overwhelm opened the door to more of my intuitive gifts.

I had spent the majority of my life, up till then, being consciously aware or "Spiritually Awake." I had studied all the spiritual books I could find as a teenager, and went into philosophy at university. I probably would have gone on a fast track into being a healer if my two soul sisters hadn't died during our teenage years. When they passed, I felt abandoned. I had survivor's guilt, as well as feeling like my soul sisters, my partners in the spiritual world, were gone. I felt my purpose had been destroyed by their deaths.

Instead of continuing down the spiritual path in my twenties, I went into the corporate world. When I found myself with not just one or two children, but four, I started asking questions in my personal Akashic Records of the Akashic Record Keeper.

The Akashic Records are a vast cosmic energy field and quantum library that preserves every thought, word, and deed from a soul's journey across thousands of lifetimes. This field contains the unique blueprint of a soul's gifts, contracts, challenges, and chosen purpose, set before birth. The Akashic Record Keepers are pure source energy beings who have never been human and offer guidance without judgment. These Beings of Light assist souls by providing ancient wisdom and healing energy to clear trauma and help individuals align with their life's highest potential.

I remember feeling like a victim needing help and thinking, *How could this happen to me? What did I do wrong to end up with four kids when I only wanted one or two?*

Of course, I'd occasionally think back to what my husband had said many years earlier when he told me that we would fill up the house. It felt like a prophecy, and likely it was, as he is tremendously intuitive and sensitive.

The Akashic Record Keepers answered my question of, "Why me?"

They told me, "You are the one who wrote contracts with all of these souls."

Well, that was a shock and really straightened out my thinking.

I didn't know much about soul contracts or having a soul plan, or even much about the Akashic Records back then. It was not a common subject in the eighties or nineties. Everything I was learning was by asking my Akashic Record Keepers. In response, I said, "What do you mean by, 'you wrote a contract with them'?"

They answered me with a lovely anecdote to explain.

They told me that before a soul comes to earth, they write many soul contracts with other souls who will be on Earth at the same time. Imagine hundreds of souls, all returning to Earth, meeting up in a huge conference room. They are all looking to complete karmic contracts, to support soul family members and other souls they've known in various incarnations. We connect and create energetic soul contracts. They told me that most of us write 50 or even 100 soul contracts.

Some of them are about support. Some of them are more about soul growth and learning. The Record Keepers call these your karmic contracts. That means you have a karmic pattern that you want to work through with that other soul.

Even if we don't have extreme Karmic patterns or contracts, it doesn't mean we don't have any learning and growth to do in this life. Some challenges and issues could be connected to a karmic pattern you've been working on over many lives. My contracts with my family were about loving support. The Record Keepers call those "support contracts."

They explained that there were four souls I had written contracts with to parent, but I had waited so long to conceive, they all had to come in quickly.

Connor came first, as an awake, present soul. I'd notice him at four months sitting up with a straight back, legs crossed, palms turned skyward—a tiny Buddha. It was so cute that I would take photos of his little hands with his palms up, and his little crossed legs and tiny feet. I started calling him my Buddha Boy. That's truly what he looked like, and it's continued to be so as a soul.

And then, when the twins had a chance to be born, they dove in together, figuring this might be their only chance. And I'm sure they were right.

Identical twins come from a single egg that splits, creating identical babies. They were girls, born eighteen months after their brother, and each had a unique soul plan. I also had a contract with my nephew.

I found it interesting when the Record Keepers explained that we don't always write soul contracts with our parents. We sometimes write a contract with a grandparent, or an aunt, uncle, or even a sibling. I'm sure my brother and my nephew had a soul contract, but it was karmic, not parental support. My nephew's main parental contract was with my parents, me, and my husband.

He moved in as a freshman in high school and was thrilled to have little siblings and a loving family who spent time with. His parents had addictive patterns, which are often karmic. It's not unusual for the children to come in with the intention that their love and light will "wake" the parents up. Helping a parent to overcome an addiction is a karmic contract. Sometimes it works, though often it doesn't. Sadly, my nephew's mom died young, and though my brother eventually got sober, he was never able to parent his son.

Parenting is complex. I have learned so much about family and what it means to parent a child from the Akashic Record Keepers, as they helped me understand and heal my life challenges.

For many, parenting truly is the greatest soul growth we ever have. Parenting taught me what real support can look like: love, patience, compassion, and releasing judgment. I've learned that children don't have to come through my body for me to love them infinitely.

Some children are born into abusive or addictive family patterns; those are often karmic contracts meant for deep growth. Many people have parents who have narcissistic tendencies or other mental challenges. We write those as karmic patterns to support those people and to learn and grow from the situations personally. Many of us grow so much from the karmic patterns in our childhood that we go on and share that wisdom with other people in a variety of ways. Some become therapists, doctors, healers, and life coaches.

When the twins were about three months old, I joined a group for "parents-of-multiples". My new best friends both had twins, and the three of us moms would take three sets of twins and older siblings out on adventures. We'd take trips to the zoo, the park, the beach, and even amusement parks and roller coasters. We had so much fun with those little kids from the time they were one year old, toddling around until they were five and off to kindergarten. That was the most joyful time of my life.

People would often ask us, when we were out, if we were a preschool because there were seven toddlers, all about the same age. We always laughed and said, "No, they're all ours." Often, people's jaws would drop open. I remember going to Snoopy on Ice every Christmas with the seven toddlers. They loved that ice skating show, and so did we.

Everybody came to our house for a playdate each week because I had childproofed it and it was safe for seven toddlers. I loved being 'the fun house', with our baby jungle gym, slides, sandbox, and swimming pool. Summer was a blast for all ten of us.

As the children grew and I continued to work in the Akashic Field, I saw soul contracts not as isolated moments but as ongoing threads in relationships. I realized I had written contracts with these souls to parent them. That recognition helped me move out of overwhelm and into purpose.

As I embraced the concept that I had written contracts with all of these souls, it truly helped me to move out of a place of victimhood into the deeper understanding that my soul's desire to fulfill this contract, in the highest way possible, is one of my soul's purposes.

So that became a huge part of my concept as a mother. My children were not just an extension of me. They had written their own soul plan with their own soul contracts, just as I had written my soul plan with soul contracts. I had also contracted with each of these "playgroup" children and their parents to help support each other as we grew.

Support contracts usually go both ways, so I would say that their contract is also about supporting me. I feel very blessed that the twins helped with my Akashic business when they were teenagers. I would often speak at spiritual expos and fairs, having a booth at these two- or three-day events, with a booth, doing readings and workshops. The twins would talk to the people who were curious about what the Akashic records were and how they could connect with them. They helped to explain some of this beautiful wisdom to the spiritual seekers who came to my booth. They always took the spiritual work that I did to heart and for granted, though they both have degrees in science. They were never doubters.

Connor had a different contract. He was always an emissary of peace—teaching friends to see a bigger perspective, offering compassion and balance. He held a higher consciousness and vibration of unconditional love, gratitude, and joy. It's interesting, as he would never actively get involved in the Expos or my work, but is always very conscious of how people feel.

He is sensitive and empathic, as are all the children and my husband, but he would teach his friends to see the bigger picture in their relationships when they were teenagers. He was always sharing beautiful wisdom, bringing guidance and understanding to his friends. Because he held a higher consciousness and a vibration of love, along with the expansive vision that there are many sides to a story, he helped his friends work through their teenage emotions with greater ease.

Still today, I believe that his bigger purpose is to hold more light, with a higher frequency of unconditional love, gratitude, and joy.

Many Lightworkers think they must find that in a job. But the truth the Record Keepers tell me is that, often, we're here to live and *be* these things… and not do them as work.

The twins made it clear early on that two souls in identical bodies are still distinct. That was an amazing epiphany for me as a spiritual seeker and teacher, to have the experience of separate souls in identical twin bodies clearly proved to me that our souls are unique. Even though they were raised exactly the same, in the very same moments, and physically, they are identical, yet their reaction to life was very different.

Lou was a happy baby, and always had a smile on her face, toddling around with her hands full of little toys as she giggled.

Orion was more challenged by being in a physical body. I remember her throwing her shoes across the room as a toddler, yelling, "Funny!" (which really wasn't funny at all, but the shoes on her feet felt funny to her). She was not comfortable in her physical form.

Clothes and shoes were uncomfortable and confined. A lot of this earthly world did not make her feel secure. Honestly, I related to her because I remember having similar feelings when I was a toddler. I had my first epiphany, that I was stuck in a body, when I was only three years old.

As the twins moved into their teens, I could see their soul contract with me and with the world more clearly. They were always supportive and loving, often making friends with kids who faced challenges and needed more encouragement and care. We even had a few of them stay with us for a short time while they sorted their traumas out with their parents.

Understanding your soul contracts can be very useful. I knew one of my bigger contracts was to help heal and release emotional trauma, and that included the twins' teenage friends.

The twins were always very close emotionally, but had very different personalities. When it came time to pick colleges, I expected them to choose a school and go together. They did most things together, and I didn't think college would be any different. I was surprised when they chose colleges at opposite ends of California.

If you're not aware of just how big California is, it takes about 20 hours to drive from one end to the other. The colleges they chose were fifteen hours apart.

As souls having a human experience, one loved the cool weather of far northern California, while the other loved the warmth and sun of Southern California.

These are truly unique choices that our souls make.

As they ventured deeper into intimate relationships, one twin realized that they did not feel very feminine. They tried different styles and looks, but never settled on one.

As toddlers, they had color-coded themselves. It made it easy for everyone to tell them apart. Lou wore pink, and Orion wore purple. And as a busy mom, it was great because I could usually find the same outfit in those two colors. They could wear their favorite color, but I didn't have to figure out two different outfits each day.

Later, their decisions moved into sexuality and intimate relationships. I supported them regardless of the form their relationships took. To me, it did not matter, straight or gay; it was their choice. As they made their choices, I continued to see them only as beautiful souls.

When we were part of the Parents-of-Multiple club, my two best friends had fraternal, boy/girl twins. Fraternal twins are much more common than identical. Fraternal twins are caused by the mother's propensity to ovulate two or more eggs at a time. That can be hereditary. Mothers pass on the gene to ovulate multiple eggs. Identical twins are not easily explained. My doctor said it is a "fluke of nature," a random, spontaneous event.

Now, one of my identical twin girls is trans male. They have been taking male hormones and even had some supportive surgery. These two souls were born as identical twin girls and have chosen to become a boy and a girl.

Soul contracts are a strong aspect of our soul's plan and inform much of our lives. According to the Akashic Record Keepers, there are possibly 1.5 billion people on Earth at this time who identify as LGBTQ (lesbian, gay, bisexual, transgender, and queer). These beautiful souls are not only working on their personal soul contracts and karmic patterns, but they are helping with the collective soul contract to rebalance Divine Feminine and Sacred Masculine energy for humanity.

I am so proud of both of these beautiful souls who honor me by calling me Mom. They live and walk in our world with love, kindness, and compassion for all of humanity. One is an archeologist, and the other is a therapist working with the LGBTQ community,

I believe, because they have been truly supported by their soul contracts with our family, they have been able to go forward and help other LGBTQ individuals to feel loved, and to work through some of their family traumas and emotional challenges. Many people have been disowned by their parents because of their sexuality and choice of sexual partners. I feel that part of my soul contract with my children is to support them as infinite souls on a human journey, and that is exactly what I choose to do every day.

Sometimes, acquaintances have asked me, "How can you be so supportive? Doesn't it upset you?" I tell them that it is not my soul path to walk, but it is my soul path to support them. I believe we are here to fully support our children as best as we are able.

As someone who spends hours a day working in the Akashic Field, the Quantum field, and the energy of Divine Source, I have been able to ask the Akashic Record Keepers many questions about soul contracts.

When I asked, "What are the biggest collective contracts on the planet now?" They answered that two of the biggest contracts are to:

Rebalance Divine Feminine and Sacred Masculine (male and female) energy. The Record Keepers told me that the world will remain out of balance until masculine and feminine can become equal.

Stop abuse of all kinds, including sexual, mental, physical, and emotional abuse.

So, I then asked them, "Why are there more transgender individuals now than ever before?"

First, let me define the word *transgender* so you understand. A transgender person is someone whose internal sense of gender (gender identity) differs from the sex they were assigned at birth, often seeking medical steps, like hormones or surgery, to align their body with their identity.

The Akashic Record Keepers explained that every human body has both male and female energy, no matter the body type. There are numerous ways to work on a collective soul contract that is about rebalancing Male and Female energy.

One way is internal. That means being conscious that you are staying in balance. If you're a woman using "male energy" at work, it would emphasize assertiveness, competitiveness, logical, goal-oriented decision-making, and structural control to drive productivity. Female energy is seen as a collaborative, empathetic, and emotionally intelligent approach, necessary for modern, innovative, and healthy work environments. When women run too much masculine energy, they often get chronic fatigue and other dis-ease in their bodies.

Many couples are working on balancing male and female energy in their personal relationships. That means aiming for equality, mutual kindness, and bringing more of the divine feminine communication, love, and compassion into the relationship. This is true for work relationships also.

Understanding the Akashic perspective deepened my understanding of my soul plan, the contracts I have with my four children, and the one I have with my husband of 35 years. That awareness doesn't erase occasional emotional moments, but those moments are fleeting. I get to spend time with two beautiful individuals who call me mom, and I'm grateful.

Parenting has taught me that souls arrive with intentions. Sometimes those intentions are to be supported, sometimes to help others heal. I believe our soul contracts are woven into daily life. The twins, who were raised consciously spiritual, absorbed those values and later used them to help others. Lou and Orion's differences—one comfortable in the body and one less so—highlighted how each soul navigates incarnation. They showed me that being raised in the same environment doesn't make people internally identical.

I'm grateful to have four children who bring love into every moment. I'm blessed to have grandchildren from my nephew and to watch our extended family grow. Being a mom of four was never what I envisioned, but my soul had greater dreams for me than I could have imagined. The work of parenting has been both my greatest challenge and my deepest joy.

Ultimately, the Akashic Records taught me that these relationships were chosen long before any of us arrived. That knowledge helped me release the drama and step into the role I'd contracted to play: a mother who loves, supports, and witnesses the unfolding of each child's unique journey. I am more than grateful for the past thirty-plus years of laughter, learning, and love—for having filled our five-bedroom house with the people my soul intended to meet.

Lisa's four kids

# Rev. Lisa Barnett

**Rev. Lisa Barnett** is the visionary founder of the Akashic Knowing School of Wisdom, a transformative platform where thousands of eager students worldwide have been guided to unlock the profound personal Soul wisdom held within their Akashic Records. As an accomplished author, Lisa has penned four insightful books on the Akashic Records, including two published in 2023: *Your Soul Has a Plan: Awaken to Your Life Purpose through the Akashic Records* and *Akasha*. Her groundbreaking work has garnered attention, and she has been featured on esteemed platforms like Gaia TV, Humanity's Team TV, and the Conscious Awakening Network TV.

With over thirty years of rich experience in Akashic Record Channeling and Quantum Healing, Lisa is dedicated to helping individuals release entrenched karmic patterns, update soul contracts, and clear limiting programs. Her expertise lies in empowering individuals to discover greater happiness, abundance, and love by aligning with their unique Soul Plan, as revealed in their Akashic Record. Through her compassionate guidance, Lisa enables profound personal transformation and enlightenment.

🌐 www.AkashicKnowing.com
📷 @akashicknowing
Scan QR code to learn more about Lisa Barnett.

# Section II:
# Becoming a Mother

- What moments in my life have asked me
  to grow in unexpected ways?

- What have I discovered about myself through
  caring for others or being deeply connected?

- Where have I learned to meet myself or others
  with greater compassion?

WE ARE CHANGED BY WHAT WE ARE
CALLED TO HOLD.

# Learning to Walk Beside My Child

*by Julia Burtseva*

I was twenty-six when my son was born. I doubt this will surprise anyone, but that was the moment my life split into *before* and *after*.

With each passing day, the questions in my head multiplied:

*What should his routine look like?*

*What should he eat?*

*How do I support and guide this new human being?*

*How do I give him as many opportunities as possible while still protecting him?*

*How do I help him find his purpose one day?*

These thoughts never really left me. And as someone prone to perfectionism, I treated motherhood like an exam—one where mistakes were not allowed and where I was determined to earn the highest possible score.

What I didn't know back then was that I wouldn't just be responsible for another life, but that I would have to rebuild my own... more than once. And I certainly couldn't have imagined that my ideas of what it meant to be an "ideal" mother would eventually shatter into countless pieces.

But first things first.

## Moving to the Other Side of the World

In my early twenties, I studied Spanish and dreamed of moving from Russia to Spain—living by the sea, waking up to sunlight, and never being in a rush. But my career, strong family ties, and the beginning of my relationship with my future husband slowly pushed those dreams into the background. At twenty-one, I got married. We bought our first apartment together, and I had no plans to move anywhere. Maybe just a week-long vacation.

Then our long-awaited son, Daniil, was born. We moved into a bigger apartment, and with it came an entirely new level of responsibility. There was little room left for youthful fantasies of a carefree life by the sea. My son was growing, I was learning to be a mother, and at some point, as often happens, a clear, seemingly reliable plan for our future formed in my mind.

As it turned out, the Universe had a different script.

My husband was offered a work project connected to the United States, and one day the question came up: *What if we moved there?*

What opportunities would it open? Would it be a good start for our child?

In life, I try to follow the principle "better to do it and regret it than not do it and regret it."

"Let's try," I said—while everything inside me tightened.

*Are we really doing this?*

My temples throbbed, and it felt like I couldn't catch my breath. After many long conversations, doubts, and careful weighing of options, we made the decision—we were moving.

At that point, all my thoughts revolved around my son. *How would he adapt? How would school go? How would he manage in a new environment, in a language he didn't yet speak?* I decided to do everything that felt within my control. I found him an English tutor. Long before the move, already having a rough idea of where we would live in California, I chose a Russian-American school for him.

I tried to control everything that seemed "controllable." If I had known then that this sense of control was an illusion, I might have saved myself a great deal of anxiety.

We packed three suitcases—one for each of us—and set off toward a new life. I clearly remember the drive to the airport. I stared silently out the window, then at the suitcases. Beside me sat my little boy, tightly holding a huge yellow Pikachu—the same one he clutched through all our flights. It still didn't feel real to me that we were actually leaving everything behind and starting over.

I believed we had a plan. Not a perfect one, but solid enough to provide a sense of safety. I thought that with enough preparation, enough foresight, uncertainty could be reduced to a minimum.

Now I understand that this was my first attempt to hold on to a plan that was already beginning to fall apart. What lay ahead wasn't just a new country or a new language; it was an experience no preparation could fully anticipate. An experience where familiar reference points disappear one by one, and you realize that the old way no longer works, while the new one hasn't yet revealed itself.

## The First Days

The first days after our arrival were not what I had imagined, and not because of what was happening around us. There was plenty of newness: a different language, unfamiliar streets, faces I didn't recognize. But inside, there was an unexpected quiet. The inner voice that usually told me what to do next seemed to go silent. I simply didn't know what would come next.

We woke up in a new house, and every morning it took me a few seconds to remember where I was. I made coffee, looked out the window, noticed a different light, different trees, a different sky, and felt as though I was learning to orient myself in the world all over again. Slowly. Carefully.

What surprised me most was how differently my son and I experienced this transition. I was always looking ahead, afraid it might be too hard for him, wondering if I'd made a mistake by taking him so far from the life he knew. He, meanwhile, lived fully in the present.

He was interested in the ducks in the pond near our home, in brightly colored packages of unfamiliar cookies at the store, and in strange words on street signs. Where I saw potential problems, he was curious.

At times, it felt like we were moving at different speeds. I was still trying to understand how everything was supposed to work, while he was already here. On this day. In this place. In what was happening right now.

Some evenings, after putting him to bed, I stayed in the kitchen longer than usual. Sitting quietly. Doing nothing. It felt important to admit, to myself, that I didn't know how things would turn out. And for the first time in a long while, I allowed myself not to know.

That feeling was unfamiliar. I had always believed that a good mother was someone who had answers: someone who planned ahead and tried to minimize risk. But here, in this new reality, that approach stopped working. The world felt too alive and unpredictable to fit neatly into a plan.

Slowly, I began to notice a change in myself. I paused more often. I watched instead of judging. I started asking not "What's the right thing to do?" but "What matters right now?"

It was during those first weeks that I began to understand something simple: motherhood isn't always about leading. Sometimes it's about walking alongside, accepting your own uncertainty, and not hiding it behind confidence. And maybe that was what allowed me to notice the small discoveries that followed.

## Everyday Discoveries

Once the initial tension eased, I had space to observe.

One of those moments happened at a playground. I watched children run, climb, and fall—and felt that familiar tension rise in me. At one point, a toddler nearby tripped. I instinctively stepped forward, ready to help, but noticed that no one else was rushing in.

The child's mother stood nearby, simply watching. Calm. Attentive. She met her child's eyes and gently said, "You're okay. You can do it. Good job!" The child stood up, brushed themselves off, and ran back to play.

I realized how hard it was for me to stay still. In the world I came from, care often meant stepping in: preventing the fall, or immediately fixing it. Here, I saw a different kind of care. Not absence, but trust. Trust in a child's ability to handle small challenges.

That moment didn't change me overnight, but it stayed with me. What if support doesn't always mean intervention? What if, sometimes, the most important thing is simply being close, while still allowing a child to have their own experience?


**A School Morning**

Every morning when my husband and I walked Daniil to school, we stayed for ten or fifteen extra minutes. He didn't rush to join the other children, and we usually waited together until the general gathering was announced.

One morning, the three of us stood there. On the playground, where the children were playing, I noticed a boy wearing two different sneakers. He jumped down from the steps and happily ran up to his teacher.

"Oh, Mrs. Ross, look how cool my sneakers are!"

The teacher smiled, agreed that they were very cool, and walked with him toward the meeting area.

I stood there with my mouth slightly open. Everything about the moment surprised me: that the parents had let their child come to school wearing mismatched shoes; that the teacher reacted so calmly; that no one seemed to see a problem at all.

I turned to my husband and quietly asked,
"Can you imagine coming to school like that?"

We looked at each other, and I suddenly realized something uncomfortable. I wouldn't have let my own child do that. Not because it was unsafe or wrong—just because *it's not how things are done*. In my childhood, the thought wouldn't even have crossed my mind.

Daniil, however, didn't find the scene surprising in the slightest.

And in that moment, I felt it clearly: how much of what I had been calling *care* was actually about my own limits, and not about his safety or freedom. How many quiet rules lived inside me? Rules that made it harder to feel free, and maybe less joyful, too.

## Traditions Week

One day, I received an email from the school announcing a week dedicated to family history and traditions. Children, together with their parents, were invited to share where they came from, what customs they had at home, and what felt important to their family. Nothing mandatory, just a few photos, an object, or a story.

As we started preparing, I suddenly realized I didn't know what to expect. I wondered how my son felt about his own "where from." Would he feel shy? Confused? Would he struggle to explain?

Daniil, on the other hand, was excited right away. He had ideas. He knew what he wanted to say and which photos we should print. When it was his turn, he calmly walked to the front of the classroom. Without rushing. He said he was born in Russia, that we speak another language at home, and that he has a grandmother who lives far away. He talked about how much he loves winter and playing in the snow. He also mentioned his favorite holiday—Maslenitsa, a week-long celebration when people make and eat lots of crepes (thin pancakes).

He spoke simply and naturally. Not trying to explain himself or to defend anything. The children listened with interest. Many asked questions. Someone said they had moved, too. The teacher thanked him in the same easy, matter-of-fact way she thanked everyone else.

As I sat there, I felt something slowly loosen inside me. I suddenly saw that so many of my worries—about being different, about not fitting in, about standing out—existed mostly in my own head. For him, his story wasn't a problem or something to smooth over. It was simply part of who he was.

That day, I understood something important: a child doesn't have to lose themselves just because they grow up between cultures. And my role isn't to hide his differences or make them more comfortable for the world, but to give them space. To support him in being himself.

**The Second Move**

The decision to move again came unexpectedly—even for us. We had lived in the United States for almost three years. Life had slowly settled into routines, friendships, and familiar rhythms. And then, suddenly, it became clear we were about to set out once more.

This time, I felt more excitement than fear. Spain. The country I had dreamed about long ago—before marriage, before motherhood, before all these turns and detours. I didn't know exactly how things would unfold, but I had a quiet sense that "it would be good."

There was a difficult conversation ahead with Daniil. I postponed it for as long as I could, as if delaying the moment when I would have to disrupt the world he had built around him. When the decision became final, we sat him down on the bed and told him we would be moving again.

He was silent: then he cried.

We didn't rush him. We just sat there with him. He talked about school, about his friends, about the things he loved: how he had only just gotten used to life there. As I listened, I understood this was no longer the small child I had once carried across borders, trying to plan everything for him. This was a person with his own experiences and attachments.

After a while, he wiped away his tears and said,
"At least I'll get to see Grandma more often."

The words surprised me with their quiet maturity. Not an attempt to comfort me, but his own way of finding something solid to hold on to.

We talked for a long time after that. About how it would be "hard." And how it was okay to miss people and feel angry. About how you don't have to be happy right away. I didn't promise that everything would be easy, and for the first time, I didn't try to convince him that this was something we *had* to do. I simply stayed with him.

Once again, we packed the same three suitcases, but this time, it felt different inside. It wasn't an escape or a leap into the unknown—it was a movement where each of us was allowed to feel differently, and still move forward together.

## An Unexpected Question

New Year's and Christmas were just around the corner. Our Christmas tree got lost somewhere in the delivery service, and the festive mood never quite arrived. Late one evening, I was working in my home office when Daniil walked in, looking unusually serious.

"Mom," he said, "I've been thinking… who do I write my letter to now?"

I looked up from my screen.

"I used to write to Father Frost," he continued. "Then in the U.S., there was Santa Claus. And today at school, I learned that in Spain, kids write letters to the Three Kings."

He paused, then smiled mischievously.
"Although… I could write to all of them. That way, I might get more presents."

At first, I felt confused. My familiar instinct kicked in—the need to explain, to clarify, to make sure everything was done the "right" way. But then it became clear that no complicated answer was needed."Write to whoever you want," I said.

He nodded, as if that was exactly the answer he'd been waiting for, and quietly left the room.

I stayed there in the silence and felt something light and simple settle inside me. My world no longer demanded choosing one thing and rejecting another. There was enough space for different traditions, stories, and ways of feeling at home.

And that was something my son had taught me.


**Living in the Present**

I don't know what comes next. Perhaps there will be new countries, new languages, and new "firsts."

What I do know is that the journey so far has changed me. Not only as a person, but as a mother. It has taught me to loosen my grip on control, to trust the process, and to see uncertainty not as a threat, but as space for growth.

I often think about who my son was at the beginning when we started our adventures—cautious, watchful, looking at the world from under his brows. And I'm struck by how much more openness, ease, and laughter I see in him now. Not because the world has become simpler, but because he has learned to feel confident within it.

Sometimes it seems to me that motherhood is less about leading and more about simply being there. Not protecting him from every fall or knowing all the answers in advance, but meeting each moment with honesty.

And perhaps that is the most valuable thing I carry with me from this journey: the understanding that we are growing together—and that maybe my son is teaching me just as much as I am teaching him.

Julia, Andrei and Daniil

## Julia Burtseva

**Julia Burtseva** is a designer and creative professional with extensive experience in editorial and visual design. Her work spans international publications and creative projects, where she focuses on structure, storytelling, and the relationship between content and form. Shaped by years of life between cultures, her perspective centers on identity, creativity, and the quiet details that influence how we see and experience the world.

○ @julano

Scan QR code to learn more about Julia Burtseva.

# 06

# "What if I'm Too Broken?"— How Motherhood Became My Greatest Healing Journey

### by Michelle Holling-Brooks

Gazing at the little being I was holding in my arms, it was hard to believe she was already a month old; she had grown so much. Soon, she would become even more interactive and show us more of her own personality and Soul's light. This thought should have brought me a sense of excitement or joy. Instead, there was an uncomfortable grip of panic and fear rising from my gut. I felt like I was about to be asked to take a universal exam for a class I didn't sign up for, and that I was going to fail miserably.

Aided by the rhythmic rocking of the chair, my daughter was drifting into a light slumber. Suddenly, my attention split, and I was witnessing myself from a very impersonal point of view. Within my mind's eye, I saw myself with a nurturing observer's lens—a mother rocking her newborn infant. From this perspective, I quickly noticed there was a sharp contrast in body language between the two beings. The infant looked to be in a state of total peace, resting in her mother's arms. Whereas the mother, myself, looked to be lost in an inner war, with a furrowed brow and a tight jaw line, sharply at odds with the softness of the infant.

Wave after wave of silent fears were emanating from her:

*What if I fail?*
*What if I try to get it right, but I'm not enough for her?*
*What if the universe made a mistake and I'm not supposed to be a mother?*
*What if I'm too broken to nurture life?*
*What if I'm fated to pass on the unresolved pains of my past to her?*

Snapping back into my body, I knew instantly that the inner conversation I'd been trying desperately to avoid and push to the side for the past nine months was no longer going to be silenced. The fears I heard coming from my field were demanding my attention. I had managed to logically justify and write off these fears as normal worries that any new parent might have, especially because I was deemed high-risk. Throughout my pregnancy, I had encountered medical challenges, so of course, it was natural to have worries that

I wasn't supposed to be a mom, to help protect myself from a potential loss or tragedy.

Yet, in that moment, I knew the conversation I'd been avoiding wasn't just the fears of whether I'd be able to bring this precious Soul into this world... after all, she was here in my arms: the fears were still a part of me just in a new shape. Ultimately, I could no longer deny the unseen fears driving me: forcing me to show up for myself and others in a way that was creating distance, detachment, and not allowing me to engage with my daughter in the way I really wanted to.

While I was meeting her physical needs (and mine), I could feel that I wasn't available for much else. My heart felt disconnected, like I was a hollow shell going through the motions. I wanted to be more for both of us, but there seemed to be an unseen obstacle in my way, and I didn't know how to change it.

At my core, I knew this feeling of separation and distance didn't start with pregnancy; it was a feeling I've felt for most of my life. The unspoken fear I had been trying to ignore for the past nine months was that I wouldn't be able to give this precious little Soul what she would really need in this world. Ultimately, what I believed was that I wasn't capable of nurturing and engaging with life in general, let alone helping to nurture hers.

Even though I had been on a healing journey for over five years at that point, there was still a huge part of me that believed the progress I'd made didn't matter. The fearful voice in my head was convinced that my past traumas and experiences were *too much*.

The core fear was that somehow I was fundamentally too broken and burdened by past generational trauma to be there for myself, let alone another being. I believed I wasn't going to be able to meet her needs. I was sure I would end up hurting her. *"Because after all,"* whispered the fearful, desperate voice within, *"that is what hurt people do... unconsciously pass on their hurt to another. You can't change that."*

As I was witnessing this inner dialogue unfold, I continued to gently rock us both. I didn't want my old trauma responses to continue to influence me behind the scenes, like a puppet master, forcing me to keep everything and everyone at a distance. After all, my belief had always been that keeping everyone at a distance would keep both me and them "safe." While I honored where these old protective beliefs came from, I didn't want to live this way anymore, especially for my daughter's sake.

A silent prayer came from my heart, *Please help me figure out how to be a nurturing mother, steward, and companion for her and for myself.*

Even as I felt this prayer, it seemed like an impossible task.

## Spirit's Invitation

Instantly, in response, I saw a simple image of a luminous linen invitation come to my mind's eye. The invitation had no writing, only a golden wax seal bearing the impression of a lotus flower. This imagery is a part of my personal shorthand with Spirit, which I began to develop when I started studying different channeling and self-work healing practices.

The Lotus flower was the symbol Spirit used to represent the Heart. Often, Spirit would guide me into the Heart to help me connect with and liberate my innermost hopes, dreams, and desires. However, today I sensed the aspects of the Heart I was going to connect with were other aspects of us that the Heart also holds: the wounded parts of us that have been exiled or deemed unworthy by our different protective mechanisms.

A part of me hesitated before opening the spiritual invitation. From past experience, I knew this type of invitation represented a bigger threshold moment into a longer journey—not just a momentary insight or "ah-ha." Whatever I was about to connect with was going to bring me into awareness with uncomfortable truths, revealing choices that parts of me would not want to make due to old protective stories. I knew it wasn't going to be a quick fix or mindset reframe. I would need to be willing to stick with whatever vision Spirit was about to offer, and let it continue to guide me through the process of creating new patterns within me; patterns that would continuously challenge my inner beliefs, each one helping me gain greater freedom and connections.

Exhaling, I silently agreed… and let it open.

As the seal on the invitation cracked, the image of a golden thread appeared. Like the string that leads a Soul through the labyrinth, the golden thread was asking me to follow into my own inner shadow world that my Heart guarded. I was being led to take down the walls that were preventing me from being who and how I wanted to be for myself and my daughter.

**First: Awareness - Honoring our Hidden Attachment Wounds**

The thread led me into a room within my Heart that looked like an art gallery. Along the walls were photos, each reflecting images from my past, creating a collection based on my history and experiences. They were all associated with the archetypal pattern of Motherhood and Mothering. The general feel of the collection was that it was a fractured and complicated connection. Exploring the photos, I recalled why it was hard for me to envision myself being a mother in the traditional sense. Between the combination of past illnesses and traumas in my early life, there were real physical barriers, as well as emotional and spiritual issues that created significant mother-wounds both personally and in general.

Pausing at a photo, I reflected on a time in my life when I had lost two family members. I recalled that it was when I had experienced my first miscarriage. The events together had frayed my already strained connections to family even more, and I had made a vow that I consciously "didn't want to pursue being a mother in this lifetime." Moving to the next photo, I saw a collage showing images of me working with clients, being with friends, connecting with the different animal companions, and communing with the land. I could sense this was where I had funnelled my maternal energy. These versions of mothering felt good to me because they were outside of the traditional roles. Turning to leave the gallery, Spirit prompted me to look again, but this time with a new perspective of seeing a manifestation of my unconscious protective fears. Looking back through the photos, I now saw that a new layer was present in each photo. There was a "film" that appeared in the space around me, distorting the field between me and everything I was connected with, especially in the last two photos.

Looking closer, just behind the film of distortion, I saw a faint outline of what looked like a collapsed young child. As I felt into her outline, I could tell she was the source of the protective film.

## Second: Connecting with the Exiles Lost in the Wounds

Spirit prompted me to continue on my journey through my Heart, following the golden thread once again. The second room felt very different. Instead of the well-organized gallery, I was inside a young, raw, tender place with my Heart. I had a sense that I'd been cut off and isolated from this part of me for quite some time.

I didn't want to be here and sensed waves of shame, even embarrassment, coming from within the room. Thinking about avoiding this room altogether, I felt a warmth of compassion and love stir within and heard Spirit say, *She needs you, be brave.*

Bracing for what might meet me, I stepped fully into the room and was surprised to find it was empty. Spirit invited me to let this room help me witness how I had (and was) showing up for my life over the past few months. I saw flashes of how I had overcome many past fears surrounding different medical traumas by being willing to seek and receive the medical help I needed and to tend to the physical needs of my body and my daughter's, something that in the past, I would not have been able to do.

Next, the room shifted to a new set of images. Within this set, I saw moments where my Heart had asked me to engage or connect with any other types of requests or guidance from Spirit that were not rooted in direct physical needs, such as emotional and spiritual needs.

Unfortunately, I had not been able to answer or engage with these in the same way. Instead, I saw the same protective "film" from the past, cutting me off once again from following my Heart's requests to connect fully. Starting to feel shame once more, Spirit reminded me to release any judgments I was experiencing in the moment. Any reflections were not to blame me, but to compassionately help reveal the hidden impact that old protective stances were actively having on me, and by default, those around me. My prayer was to heal these wounds, and healing always starts with loving awareness.

The tender awareness brought forward the truth that my fears had, and were, costing me precious moments and experiences. I was actively shielding, keeping my Heart at a disconnected protective distance, and this was robbing me of the love that could be present. As the images dissolved, a knowing washed over me; if I left this pattern unhealed, it would continue to steal any future experiences and moments of connection from myself and my daughter.

The room changed once again. This time it wasn't an image that came forward, but the revelation that there was a small child crouched in the corner at the back of the room, the same one I had seen as a faint outline in the photos. Between us was a pile of bricks, forming a massive wall. Knowing she represented my inner wounded child, I wanted to go to her. Spirit asked me to pause and look at the bricks first. Studying them, I noticed they had labels on them like: outcast, unwanted, loner… and so on. Touching the different bricks, I felt the different experiences each brick represented. I could feel the unseen ways these wounds were currently and silently restricting and preventing me from connecting with pretty much any part of my life, in the way that felt aligned with my true self—physically, emotionally, mentally, and spiritually.

Waves of my own fear tore at me, standing in that room, witnessing my own inner wounded child and the impact that aspect of me was having on my life. I was worried that somehow I would pass this same heart-wall on to my child. Once again, I wanted to let go of the golden thread and stop the vision. Before I could, the little one in the corner materialized another larger brick that read: *I'm broken, and I break others, too.* She truly believed she was past the point of being able to heal. A wave of deep compassion erupted from my heart for this little child, and for my own self as a child. I didn't want her to stay crouched in a corner of shame and fear. I wanted her to remember that she, and everyone, is always worthy of love and acceptance—no matter what has happened in the past.

Crawling over the wall between us, I sat down next to her and gently offered her my attention and care. As I did this, Spirit reminded me this was something *I did know how to do.* I saw another set of images: all the ways, over the past few years, that I was already healing the wounds held within me. I wasn't always this little, walled-off, wounded child anymore. And as the last photo in the gallery had shown me, I was finding a new way to connect. And yes, even though I still had parts of me guarding themselves, I was actively trying to stop pushing people away.

I had formed a life with a partner, friends, and now a new little one. I had already stopped building my walls as high and wide. Looking back to where the wall had been just moments before, it was now dissolving, becoming lower and lower. Standing up, the child by my side took my hand and stood up, too. Together, we stepped over the wall and followed the thread into the final room of our Heart that Spirit wanted us to visit today.

## Third: Awakening to the Soul Medicine of Nurturing

I knew the final room well. It was where I came to connect with Soul Medicine. In this room, I was transported to a meadow of lush grass that held a drinking well that would fill with whatever Medicines of the Soul would best serve myself or another, when I was prompted to ask for Spirit's support.

Approaching the well, I saw a label I hadn't worked with before, *Nurturing*. Sitting at the foot of the well, drinking and feeling into the energy of nurturing, I saw how it could interweave with my prayer of asking for Spirit's support to be a nurturing mother. An inner truth illuminated with my heart space; to be nurturing, I didn't have to do anything but be willing to be with, to open to, and listen. This soul-level truth was challenging the idea my ego-self had formed; *to be a good mother or nurturer, I have to do all the "right" things.* Rather, as I sat next to the well, I understood that to be a nurturing mother, I simply had to be willing to be with both myself and the other just as we were, rooted in the same love and compassion I had just offered to the little one by my side.

The universal Soul Medicine of Nurturing is at the heart of the archetypal pattern of Mother. It is the Soul Medicine that a Mother freely offers in many different ways. Through attuned nurturing of a mother, in all the forms that might take, we can soften our fears, cultivate courage, and shift from being disengaged and restricted in our lives, to allow and be in co-creation with the fullness of life. This was the medicine that would help me answer my prayer, transcending past pains and fears, so that I could meet myself and my daughter with attuned care and connection.

Looking at my own inner child sitting next to me at the well, she was no longer feeling lost in inner wounds. She was ready to celebrate, dance, laugh, even play in the meadow… and with the world again.

## Flowing with the Medicine of Nurturing

My focus shifted from my inner world back to my outer senses. Looking down at my daughter held in my arms, I felt a thread of connection coming from within that hadn't been there before. There was a sliver of hope: it might be possible to shift from what felt like a hollow shell going through the motions to engaging in mothering.

Before closing out my vision, there was one last stop for me. Spirit prompted me to check in again with both my own physical body and my daughter's to see what might be different now.

I sensed her body first. It was truly soft and visually reflecting signs of safety, trust, belonging, and love. She was not only letting me hold her, she was completely softening into my arms and chest. Even more shocking to me was that I noticed that my body was not actually pulling away or holding signs of the tightness or tension I had previously felt. My facial muscles had softened, and a gentle smile was emerging from my lips. My body was perfectly attuned to, and moving with, her request for connection, engaging with her, aligned with mutual trust.

Just then, she stirred in her sleep, reaching out her little hand into the air, searching and knowing that an attuned touch would answer her. I felt my body naturally start to reach back toward her, answering her request. Then a different part of me questioned the response. Freezing mid-reach, I knew where the hesitation was coming from, my own inner child. Quickly, I looked inward and found her back in the second room (the dark, isolated room), standing at the remnants of the wall. She looked concerned that somehow she would be hurt or hurt someone. I felt a nurturing spirit come up to her and say, "It's okay, you are safe. We can reach back, we can answer her, it will be okay…"

She replied back, "But I don't know how."

Suddenly, I knew the answer for both her and me. I didn't know how to reach back from a mental point of view, but my Body and Heart already knew how. While my mind and ego-self had been lost in trauma response stories rooted in past experiences, as soon as I softened my attachments to the authority the old wounds had over me and tended to them with love and compassion, my Body's innate healing wisdom was able to instantly respond. I didn't consciously tell or make my body do anything. Instead, once I released the hold that fear had over me, my own body was free to move from love, not fear.

My body had automatically answered my daughter's request without my ego telling it what to do. I felt almost weightless with joy; the old narrative, that because of my past traumas, I was broken and did not know how to connect, simply wasn't true.

The image of the invitation came back to me, but this time with a question. *"Michelle, are you willing to stay open to this thread and continue to learn how to be nurtured and mothered by love?"*

Softening and letting out my breath, I answered, *Yes.* My hand reached out to her little fingers. They clasped my index finger, pulling my hand into her chest and burrowing a little deeper into my own chest.

Tears gently rolled down my cheek, and I felt a visceral sensation of connection flowing even more from my heart to hers and back again: a true first for me with another human being.

## Prayer for Nurturing

While we continued to rock, I knew this was a moment of awakening and that the real work lay ahead of me. I understood that I was likely to get lost again, separated from this connection. And I knew in those moments, all I needed to do was look for and follow this same golden thread, so it could lead me back to connecting with the medicines of mothering, nurturing, and connection.

I said another prayer for support and asked for help:

*Please, help to remember I am my own Mother, I have the power to nurture within. Help me remember that I can always ask for Spirit's help, and the same golden thread will continue to connect me with the parts of me that are lost. Help me remember that this medicine is always within me, and if I forget, that my Body remembers the way there, too. Help me continue to trust in my Body's wisdom to guide me in, through, and connect with my true self.*

***

Seventeen years of traditional and unconventional experiences of motherhood later, and I'm happy to share that my vision that day in the rocking chair has helped me cultivate a tangible willingness to seek the Soul Medicine of nurturing anytime I feel disconnected or lost in fear.

Over the years, I have had to follow the golden thread back through these three rooms of my Heart Being many times. Each pass through, I see, feel, and witness different parts of me that are lost in trances of separation and fear, emerging with greater wholeness and alignment with who I truly want to be for myself and for those I am being asked to hold within a nurturing space.

I now call the practice that Spirit gave me that day the "Golden Thread of Nurturing: Moving Through Separation to Union."

If it feels good to you, I invite you to create your own version of the golden thread practice, so that you, too, can discover a similar practice to support you in mothering the different parts of you that need nurturing, so you can, in turn, pass the same blessings on to others in your life.

I invite you to re-read my story, and this time let Spirit guide you on your own vision quest at the same time. Let Spirit guide you into your own inner chambers of your Heart, following the golden thread of connection to the medicines of your Soul. You might also consider taking this same golden thread with you as you read through this book, letting it help you gather new medicines, jewels, while organically reconnecting you with the archetypal healing power that comes and is held within our sacred bonds as child, as mother, and as nurturer, in all the forms that might come in.

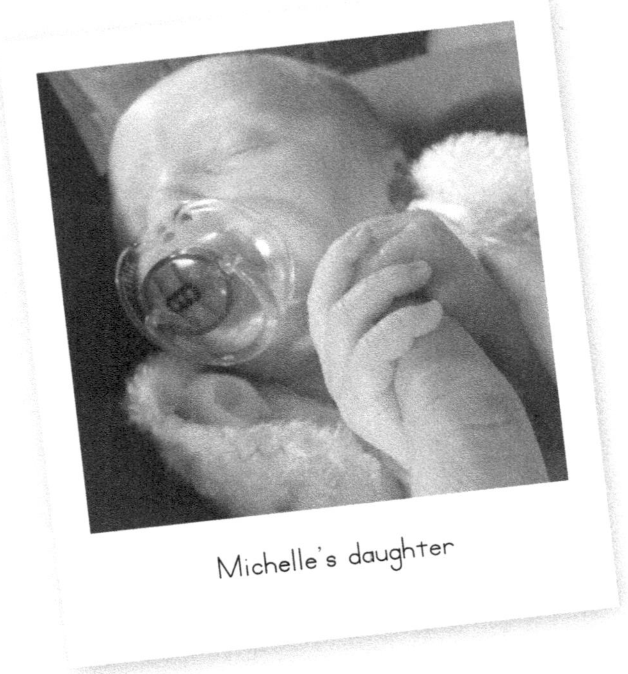

Michelle's daughter

# Michelle Holling-Brooks

**Michelle Holling-Brooks** shares more stories and sample practices on how to cultivate deeper connection with mothering and nurturing growth into one's true self in her book *Trauma Informed Enlightenment: Awakening to the Healing Power of the Sacred Witness*. The book also has a companion Oracle Deck and Guidebook, *The Sacred Witness Oracle*.

Together, these three sacred tools serve as a soul companion for those seeking to become a healing presence for themselves and others—physically, emotionally, mentally, and spiritually. Additional healing wisdom and free resources are available on her website.

⊕ www.UnbridledChange.org

◎ @unbridled.change

Scan QR code to learn more about Michelle Holling-Brooks.

# 07

# The Gift

*by Molli Burkett*

One of the greatest gifts I've ever received came from my children.

Did they set out to give me this gift?
Were they aware they were giving it?

I really don't think so.

And yet, it remains the most precious gift a mother could ever receive—one I will carry with me always, with deep gratitude.

I was a single mother to three wonderful children. Our life was imperfect and at times deeply challenging. We struggled. We made mistakes. And yet, we found our way. The love between us was real and deep, and my bond with each of them was strong, distinct, and alive. My guiding focus was always my children—creating as much safety, love, and steadiness as I could.

Although it was difficult, we also had a lot of joy. Hot Arizona days were spent in the pool and around the barbecue. Pizza nights, board games, and movies were punctuated by belly laughs—along with the occasional argument, of course; we were a family.

Their father and I divorced when the children were just one, three, and five years old. The divorce was incredibly difficult for them. The marriage had been toxic, and both of us played a part. I was not well after the split, though I hadn't been well before it either. In truth, I had not been well for much of my life.

Not long after the divorce, I recognized that I needed help recovering from alcoholism and depression. I committed to doing my own inner work, supported by groups, mentors, and healers of many kinds. As I moved toward healing and wholeness, I remember when a lightbulb moment came: *I could not be fully present for my children unless I first learned how to be present for myself.*

It was a slow unraveling—one that continues still. A careful unpeeling of layers that once kept me safe, yet also concealed the truest version of who I am: the self buried beneath expectations, roles, and a life shaped more by others' dreams and ideas for me than my own.

Through a spiritual awakening, I learned, painful as it was, that I had to look at myself with total honesty. With the dawning of awareness came the possibility of healing an inherited disconnection shaped by generations of conditioning. From there, I began to slowly step into the person my Higher Power had always intended me to be.

As I slowly began to "come home" to myself, the quiet blessings of growth, softening, and compassion rippled outward, very gradually, through our family life.

Like so many parents, my intentions were good, and my love for my children ran deep. I longed to show them that they came first. Through my own personal growth work, I began to understand what emotional availability could look like, and I deeply wanted to offer that to them.

My kids and I were tight. As they grew, I would share with them, in an age-appropriate way, about my history with alcoholism and mental health issues. I educated them on how addiction runs in families, the importance of talking about things, and receiving outside help.

I passed along what I was learning: sometimes through conversation, sometimes simply through how I lived. Spiritual connection was welcomed in our home, and I encouraged them to explore their own relationships with meaning, faith, and curiosity. I did the very best I could with what I had.

And I had a lot.

Because of my healing journey, I had amazing mentors and friends who felt like sisters and who truly wanted the best for me. I had resources all around me, and I drank them in (pardon the pun). As people showed up for me, I showed up for others and myself. The huge bonus was that I started learning how to be present and show up emotionally for my kids.

Like most teenagers, mine were not immune to experimentation, missteps, and the inevitable bumps that come with growing into adulthood. I laugh now when I think about how certain I was that my openness about addiction and its dangers would somehow shield them from those very experiences. I truly believed that my awareness and recovery had given me a kind of parental advantage.

As my children grew into young adults, our family dynamic shifted. We were no longer the "Four Musketeers." Each child was navigating their own world, and their individual struggles often clashed. They each had their own hopes, interests, dreams, and ideas about life. I desperately wanted to keep us together. I offered advice. I jumped into arguments and tried to smooth things over, often becoming exasperated in the process.

Over time, although we remained connected, I noticed a growing emotional distance. I knew, intellectually, that this was normal. Children are meant to grow up and move outward. I encouraged them to fly, after all. And yet, I felt hurt. Where we had once been so close, there was now tension and withdrawal.

Friends reassured me: "They're cutting the apron strings in their own way." Still, I felt grief and resentment. I didn't understand what had happened.

One was still living at home while the others moved in and out, coming and going through the rhythm of their own lives. They had grown, and the way they related to one another had begun to shift. My daughters became really close friends as young adults: it was really beautiful to watch as they became confidants to each other while spending a great deal of time together. My son was going through his own struggles, and our relationship was somewhat strained. I began to notice that they wanted to spend less time with me, and that when we were together, I often felt a sense of annoyance. I chalked it up to the normal differentiation process young adults go through. Yet in my heart of hearts, I sensed that it was more than that.

Then, one day, one of my children, who had once shared everything with me, opened up to me again. She spoke vulnerably about something painful. I listened. I tried to provide comfort. And then I pointed out all the good things she had going for her and how she didn't need to feel the way she was feeling.

She looked at me and said, **"Don't invalidate me."**

It landed like a bolt of lightning.

In that moment, the sky seemed to clear, and I saw myself and our dynamic with new clarity. Yes, I was willing to listen. Yes, I cared deeply. But I began to wonder: *could I allow her to have her feelings without trying to change them? Could I sit beside her in her pain without stepping into the role of the rescuer?*

She didn't need me to *make* her feel better; she needed compassion, empathy, and understanding. I could see then that my instinct to ease the discomfort, for both of us, came from love, even as it pulled me away from what I most wanted to offer: presence and emotional availability.

Looking back, I can see where I had believed—quietly, unconsciously—that I had some control over their process and that they needed me to take on that role.

I had learned a great deal in my personal growth journey about the drawbacks of offering unsolicited advice to other adults: a long-held habit I had worked hard to release. And yet, when it came to my adult children, I still believed they could benefit from my input on at least the really *important* things… right? I felt I *knew* what they might want to consider in order to stay safe, grounded, and care well for their future selves. After all, I had an abundance of life experience; *surely my young adult children should benefit from my hard-earned wisdom.*

I was the fixer. If I didn't have the answer, I would find it. If my children were uncomfortable, I wanted to remove the discomfort. I tried to protect them from choices that might lead to pain or discomfort. I wanted them to make the "right" decisions, so their future would be secure.

Isn't that what parents do?

Guide their children toward safety, stability, emotional and spiritual well-being? But wait…they weren't children…

Clarity began showing up everywhere. I found myself gently questioning assumptions I hadn't even realized I was holding. I believed I was open to my children pursuing their dreams—but was I really?

I began to notice a quiet condition beneath that openness. As long as I didn't perceive their choices as dangerous or potentially painful, I could support them with ease. But when something felt risky to me, I would offer alternatives, suggest other paths, or slowly withdraw from the conversation, hoping my lack of encouragement might nudge them away from what I feared, toward safer choices.

At the time, it felt like care. Looking back, I can see how curiosity often gave way to caution, and how presence sometimes quietly turned into avoidance.

And then a deeper question emerged: if they were adults, could they make these decisions for themselves? What message was I sending when I stepped in? I began to see that, despite my loving intentions, I may have been communicating doubt: about their ability to discern, to stay safe, or to trust themselves.

I began to question my own certainty. Just because something felt unsafe to *me*, did that truly mean it was wrong for *them*? Did I really have the answers I thought I did? Was it possible that my fear, shaped by my own experiences, was getting in the way of their unfolding?

And in that wondering came a humbling realization: perhaps they, too, were guided by something greater than me. Perhaps they had their own relationship with a Higher Power… and it didn't require *my* intervention.

I recognized that although my own healing journey shaped how I had parented and what I brought to our family, it didn't change the fact that they were on their *own* journey, a path that was all their own.

I began to sit with this and reflect on how it felt to be on the receiving end of my "helpful" responses. When I have a meaningful plan, dream, or goal, what happens inside me if someone immediately points out why it might not be a good idea? I notice anger arise, and when I look more closely, I see what's underneath it. Shame. The quiet shame of not feeling respected or validated. The shame that settled in when my own ideas began to feel silly, unrealistic, and unworthy.

In those moments, when met with those types of responses from people, I often felt unseen, as though my voice and inner knowing about my own life didn't quite matter. Over time, those past experiences had led me to shut down, to pull inward, and to feel deeply alone. It had also caused resentment toward that person who was behaving in this way toward me. *Could this be part of the annoyance and resentment my young-adult children seemed to feel toward me?*

I began working with this intentionally, knowing it would take practice. I stumbled many times. When I felt a strong urge to offer advice or input to one of my adult children, especially when it hadn't been asked for, I practiced pausing instead. When their plans, dreams, goals, or interests stirred fear in me, I learned to notice my feelings and stay quiet.

Sometimes that meant taking a walk to create space between myself and the impulse. Other times, it meant reaching out to a mentor or a friend walking a similar healing path, giving voice to thoughts I knew might not be appropriate to share with my children. I shared openly with those who understood the work I was doing—mentors, friends, and professionals who could offer honest reflection without judgment. Again and again, I was gently reminded that restraint, too, could be an act of care, and that not every opinion needs to be spoken to be held with love.

Each time I felt the urge to control an outcome, I practiced noticing it: without judgment, self-criticism, or shame. Just noticing and refraining from taking any action on it.

As I practiced restraint, something shifted inside me. The feelings followed the behavior. As fear softened, genuine curiosity began to emerge in its place. I found myself wondering what they loved about a particular idea, what fascinated them about an interest, and how it felt in their bodies to imagine reaching a goal or bringing a dream to life.

By opening myself this way, I began learning who my children were on a much deeper level. When I stopped trying to keep them "safe" from what *I believed might hurt them,* or from ideas I thought weren't wise, I was freed to truly hear them: their hearts, their minds, their dreams, and their desires. When I held back on the unsolicited advice or quiet control, they could make their own mistakes and learn their own lessons.

As I kept my mouth shut and my ears open, I noticed that, over time, my judgment about what I thought they should or shouldn't be doing began to soften. In that letting go, I became an emotionally safe person for them to simply be themselves. The less I believed I "knew" what was best, the more they opened up, sharing their mistakes, joys, highs, and lows.

If they loved to drink champagne, I could enjoy that moment with them, even if I chose not to drink. If they made choices about romantic partners that I wouldn't have made for myself, I learned to let go, stand beside them in their choices, and trust their unfolding without needing to hold judgment. I stopped watching out for them and began simply being with them.

What I hadn't understood before the Gift was that as my children moved into adulthood, they no longer needed me to ensure their safety or well-being. What they truly needed was to be seen, validated, understood, and trusted. They craved attunement, but in an adult way.

At the time, I couldn't see that the more I interfered through unasked-for input, unspoken judgments, or careful explanations of why their choices might or might not be a good idea, the more distance it created between us.

My intentions, like those of so many parents, were loving and sincere. I wanted what was "best for them.: I wanted them to be safe and to live full, meaningful lives. Yet, by not allowing them the space to have their own paths, goals, ideas, and to make their own mistakes, I was unintentionally contributing to resentment and separation. I was also, without realizing it, stepping into territory that wasn't mine to occupy. They had their own inner guidance, their own Higher Power… and that presence was not me.

In my desire to protect my adult children, I had become emotionally unsafe. I unintentionally taught my children to be careful about what they shared with me. Without realizing it, I had communicated that certain thoughts, plans, or feelings weren't safe to bring into our conversations because I always had a lot to say, much of it offered with love, but much of it experienced as invalidating.

They also learned to be cautious with their emotions. I had a habit of trying to fix or change *how they felt,* and in doing so, they were often left feeling unseen or misunderstood. When they shared feedback about my behavior, especially when it stirred discomfort in me, I sometimes became defensive instead of fully listening.

Over time, this led to frustration on both sides, and each of them found their own way of responding. One pulled back and shared less, visibly irritated when I spoke. Another escaped altogether. One became so angry that there were times we hardly spoke, and when we did, it often ended in conflict.

It took time to rebuild trust. I owned my behaviors with them and made amends for any harm I may have unintentionally caused. But they needed to see it, feel it, trust it over time.

The unsolicited advice mostly stopped (sometimes I slip—I'm human). When they came to me and shared, I learned to ask whether they were looking for input or simply needed to vent. I opened myself to the possibility that I didn't always know what was best. That I couldn't be certain which choices were right or wrong for them. I acknowledged that they were allowed to discover who they were, what they wanted, and how they felt as adults.

I became someone who could sit with their feelings, with compassion, empathy, and love, without dismissing, invalidating, or trying to fix them. Over time, my opinions and judgments softened in my own mind. That was how I knew the change was real. I no longer had to hold my tongue the way I did in the beginning, because the advice wasn't rushing in anymore. I wasn't fighting it off; it simply wasn't there.

By honoring my children's feelings and creating distance, they, in turn, gave me the gift of a lifetime: the opportunity to grow into an emotionally safe person. Today, they share so much more of their lives with me. They enjoy my company because there is space for them to simply be themselves: seen, appreciated, and respected for who they are. They can speak freely and share their interests, dreams, and opinions without worrying about how I might respond. And instead of judgment, they get to feel my genuine excitement, compassion, curiosity, empathy, and joy about what they are experiencing and who they are becoming.

I've worked with many people who feel as though they have "lost" their children. When parents try to protect and guide their adult children, it is most often rooted in love and good intentions. Yet, for the adult child on the receiving end, it can sometimes feel the opposite.

Ah… but all is not lost! When we are willing to look at our relationships from a different perspective, to honestly explore how even our well-intentioned behaviors and ideas may be creating distance, there is real hope for change. If you find yourself in this place with your adult children, know this: it is never too late.

The work may not be easy. It can require gently peeling back layers that have been in place for a long time, so you can see what is truly happening beneath the surface. It may involve imagining what it feels like to be on the receiving end of behaviors meant to help or protect. At times, this process can be painful. Rebuilding trust often takes time, but it *can* be done. I have witnessed it again and again, and it is my own lived experience.

At their core, families want to be connected, but they often don't know how. When unintentional emotional "unsafety" is present, grown children may choose distance, because staying close leaves them feeling hurt, frustrated, unvalidated, or unseen. Sometimes those patterns are even repeated by the adult child in response. In these moments, the only work truly within our control is our own—to take responsibility for our part, to repair where possible, and to shift the patterns that may have made us feel unsafe to those we love.

If you are struggling in this way, please take heart. The journey ahead may feel wild at times, filled with reflection, uncovering, and discovery. Yet, on the other side, there may be an unexpected gift: the gift of becoming an emotionally safe person, and with it, the possibility of a depth of emotional intimacy with your adult children that you may have once believed was lost.

For those who have not yet received the gift of meeting your adult children right where they are—within an honest, respectful, and continually evolving relationship—my prayer is that this gift is given to you now. For it is among the most joyous, beautiful, and sacred gifts a parent can ever receive.

Molli Burkett and her kids

# Molli Burkett

**Molli Burkett** is a trauma-informed Somatic Coach who supports people in breaking free from family and cultural conditioning. The Greek word *Soma* refers to the body as a whole—embracing all of who you are. It is often understood as experiencing the body from a felt, living, and conscious perspective. The body carries its own deep intelligence that the mind alone cannot access. When the Soma is fully integrated, the mind discovers true freedom.

Through her transformative approach, she is dedicated to empowering individuals to release old patterns, narratives, and behaviors shaped by the imprint of family dysfunction and trauma. This approach fosters a beautiful reclamation of the authentic self.

Time and again, Molli has witnessed how embracing an embodied way of living cultivates self-trust, deeper self-connection, and genuine self-love. This profound alignment results in healthier, more meaningful relationships–not just with ourselves, but in every aspect of life, from love and family to work and play. It's a shift that has the potential to transform life at its core.

⊕ www.MolliBurkett.com
◎ @molliburkettcoaching
Scan QR code to learn more about Molli Burkett.

# 08

# A Mother the Color of Blue

*by Trish Leichty, MD*

On a particularly loud day—grandchildren squealing, dogs nudging, everyone wanting something from me—I did what I often do when I want to disappear from the present moment and slip into my imagination. I opened Zillow.

During this crowded season, scrolling through listings had become a strange kind of meditation for me. A quiet fantasy of solitude. A vision board for a peace I couldn't quite name.

That's when I saw it.

A little blue cabin held on the expanse of Wyoming land. The exact deep blue of my bedroom walls and half of my home. The kind of blue that feels like dusk—soft, grounded, infinite. My heart skipped. I must have looked through those pictures a dozen times: zooming in on the porch, the view from each window, the adorable kitchen.

I saved the property, of course, but didn't think much of it.

Dogs were begging to be fed, emails were waiting to be responded to, and a bunch of humans downstairs were wondering where I had been for the past 45 minutes.

Sighing deeply as I put my phone down, I thought to myself, *Get it together, Trish.* A few weeks later, as I was increasingly snapping at the dogs, impatient with my husband, and constantly on the verge of tears, I realized that things were catching up with me. Our third of four children had recently moved out of the house, leaving us with one child left to parent. I had been simultaneously grieving her absence while looking forward to having more space in my life after mothering for the past twenty-eight years.

And then, unexpectedly, our adult son and his family moved in with us.

Instead of grieving in the solitude of my home and enjoying peaceful dinners with my husband and our remaining daughter, we now had additional people and pets living with us. Was it any wonder why I was dreaming on Zillow about a Little Blue Cabin in the middle of Wyoming?

On impulse, I booked a hotel near where my oldest daughter had recently moved and began packing the few things I needed. "Grandma, whatcha doing?" My precocious five-year-old granddaughter asked as she followed me curiously around the house. "I'm going to visit Lacy for a few days, Sweets. I promise to give her a big squeeze from you."

Satisfied with my answer, she smiled and skipped away, leaving me to finish my packing. As I folded my favorite pjs and placed them in my bag, I felt both sadness and gratitude that I could not yet understand.

Two podcast episodes later, I pulled into the hotel parking lot, thrilled to be just a few moments away from crawling into bed. The silence in my hotel room felt strange at first. Then delicious. I snuggled under the covers, poured some wine in a paper cup, and opened a bag of cheese popcorn—a small rebellion in a life of constant tending.

I looked around the room. The modern artwork on the walls, the worn carpet beneath the bed. How often do I just sit and simply observe? If my body isn't in motion, my mind sure is. A nonstop conversation with a thousand voices. I continued to sit there in silence, beginning to feel my own energy again. The hum of my heartbeat. The soft ache behind my ribs.

My thoughts drifted back to my house full of people—my son, his wife, their three kids, the dog—all living with us. And I wondered, *Why did I do this? Why, when given the chance to finally have more of myself, did I take this on?*

Of course, I was grateful for the opportunity to help them, but I was also exhausted. Frustrated. And sad that it was so easy for me to rush to take care of others instead of slowing down to see what I needed. This pattern had followed me my entire life, especially with this particular son.

He and I share a long, tangled history. The kind of bond built not just on love, but on trauma and guilt, inherited pain and unspoken apologies. From his first flutter in my womb, our story began inside betrayal. His father's abuse and affair. My silent knowing. The way I carried fear in my body while carrying him.

Even as a physician, I didn't understand trauma then—the way it imprints itself into tissues, cells, generations.

I only knew that from the beginning, I felt like I had to make it up to him. To mother him perfectly, to protect him from every echo of that first wound, and every hurt that followed. Which means I spent decades trying to fix what was never mine to fix.

Decades carrying shame disguised as devotion. Fear pretending to be love. No wonder he came back home.

At twenty-six, with a family of his own, he moved into my house like a mirror I couldn't ignore. A final curriculum I needed to learn. It was as if life was giving me another chance to love without rescuing.

In the quiet of that hotel room, under the night of the Scorpio new moon—a season of shadows and rebirth—I realized that this pain still lived in me. Hidden but alive. Taking up space in my body that felt heavy and solid, separating me from my joy.

And then, unexpectedly, a voice inside whispered, *What is the one thing you want the most that has nothing to do with anyone else? The thing you're ashamed to ask for?*

Surprisingly, an image of the little blue cabin nestled on that precious land popped into my mind. The voice whispered again. *Go see it.*

I laughed out loud at the ridiculousness of this suggestion, "Yeah, right!" Of course, the practical questions showed up immediately, dressed in worry. *With what money? What will my husband say?*

But the voice persisted: *Your desires are worth stepping into. Just for you. Even if it leads nowhere, allow yourself to want.*

Taking all of this in, I kept hearing *go see it, go see it* like an echo bouncing off the walls of my mind. My heart pounded in my chest, my palms sweaty as I opened Zillow. There she was, still for sale. The same deep blue, the same porch overlooking the sweetness of the earth, waiting with open arms.

Throwing my phone to the side, I jumped off the bed, shaking my arms, and paced around the room. "This is crazy!" I said out loud. The inner war was instant—logic versus longing, shame versus soul.

*Get in your body. Stay with your breath.*

Taking deep inhales and exhales, I slowed my breathing while swaying gently, as if soothing a baby in distress. I walked over to my phone and slowly picked it up. One last deep inhale as I filled out the request form, hovering over the submit button, as if it might bite.

And then something shifted. My chest softened, my breath released, and I pressed "Send."

It felt like the smallest rebellion—a scandalous prayer.

Within minutes, my phone buzzed. The realtor confirmed my appointment for the next evening. *Holy cow. What did I just do? This is crazy!*

But underneath the chatterbox in my head, I felt the approving nod of my heart. I had followed the breadcrumbs of my own desire without justifying it to anyone—not even myself.

Sitting across from my daughter the next morning at breakfast, I was unsure if I should share what I'd done. I watched her crystal blue eyes dance as she talked about applying to law school, her cats, and how much fun she was having in her new Wyoming home. Hearing the joy in her voice, my thoughts drifted to all the women in my life.

Each one was brilliant, independent, hard-working, and highly devoted to their jobs and families. And yet I could not remember ever seeing joy in their eyes. I did not have one memory of feeling peace in their presence.

That is not what I want for my daughters. Heck, that isn't what I want for myself! I slid my phone across the table and showed her the picture on Zillow.

"Mom, that is the cutest place! I think it's so cool you're going to see it." Relieved that she didn't think I was crazy, I asked if she would go with me. "I can't wait!" she said. I could feel that she meant it.

On the drive that evening, I felt alternating waves of excitement, shame, and fear. I kept reassuring myself that the outcome didn't matter because the purpose was to allow myself to have this adventure for the joy of it. I was being invited to play with the Universe.

The last several miles were on a gravel road surrounded by ancient boulders, grazing cows, and acres of earth. The sun was beginning its descent for the day, painting the sky with pastel watercolors. I literally squealed with delight, "Oh my gosh… look at this magic!"

The cabin was smaller than I expected, but it radiated warmth. Each room was cozy and bright. Every window revealed views that took my breath away.

Lacy and I stepped onto the back porch, overlooking the endless rolling hills, and a family of grazing deer stopped to look up at us. My breath caught in my chest, and I turned to look at my daughter, who smiled knowingly. It felt as if she was part of a cosmic secret I hadn't yet been privy to.

There was no booming spiritual epiphany, no sign from the heavens—just a deep, cellular knowing that this place had been waiting for me all along.

The realtor was talking about property lines and septic systems, but I barely heard him. I was busy listening to something else entirely—the rhythm of the wind through the trees, the heartbeat of the earth, the faint sound of my own laughter returning. And an ancient voice within that whispered, *Welcome home, baby.*

Of course, I couldn't make an offer on the cabin that day. I had no idea how it would ever be possible. But I did know this was the beginning of a wild adventure.

Two months later, when the papers were signed and the keys were in my hand, I walked through each room, touching every wall, stopping to look out every window.

*Thank you,* I whispered, over and over.
To the walls.
The floorboards.
The wooden ceiling above.
To God. The Earth. To myself.

Next, I went outside to the land, and as I walked its perimeter, each step felt as if we were greeting each other for the first time. *Hello, new friend. Or maybe... hello again.*

Although I could not yet live here full-time, I felt I was finally home.

Shortly after we closed, I excitedly planned my first extended stay at Little Blue Cabin. I felt like a pregnant mom nesting—making lists, buying things at thrift stores, and dreaming of what it would be like to stay there.

But as I began packing the car for my trip, a familiar tangle of shame and guilt began to wrap its way around me. The tug of war between feeling responsible for the people I loved and the intense longing to be by myself has followed me from daughter to doctor, wife to mother.

I was beginning to see just how deeply my identity had been built on "care taking." Putting myself first felt not just foreign, but wrong. *You don't have to go. You could stay.*

*No.* I heard. *Not this time. This time I'm choosing me.*

As I drove away, my grip on the steering wheel loosened. My breath deepened, and tears rolled down my face as a quiet wisdom rose like prayer:

*You are not abandoning anyone. You are finally choosing not to abandon yourself.*

The messages kept coming, like a mother I'd always needed finally speaking:

*When you never get a break from others—when you're constantly doing and giving—you lose your connection to yourself. You forget what your own voice sounds like. You forget what it feels like to just be you.*

*You've lived your whole life entangled in energy that isn't yours. It's time to remember what brings YOU life. What is YOURS to feel.*

*It's time to learn to be alone… to hear your own words, to feel your own feelings, and to make space to birth your own dreams from the stillness.*

*As you feed yourself through solitude, no one in your life will be starved of your love. They will be fed by the overflow.*

I cried the entire drive. Grief, longing, relief. Years of waiting for permission to finally say, *This is for me.*

From this moment on, Little Blue Cabin began to teach me things no therapist, teacher, or training ever had. She taught me how to rest without guilt. How to listen without fixing. How to let the earth mother me when I was tired of mothering everyone else.

It wasn't the kind of healing that needed my hard work and effort—it was the kind that showed up simply through my dreams at night, through the wind, water, deer, and sky. Little Blue Cabin quieted the world so I could hear myself again.

*I can't live like this anymore.*
*I just want to be free.*
*To move slower. Rest. Do less.*
*I want to dance, smell flowers, walk the land, be with animals, and soak in the sun.*
*I want to trust the Universe to show up and provide everything I need.*
*I want to have fun.*

I began to see how the life I'd built—degrees, marriage, motherhood, ministry, medicine—was crafted from blueprints I didn't design. Even healing had become another performance. Another attempt to earn love by working hard and helping others.

These moments that I spent with Little Blue Cabin and the land were like a womb that held me as I found my way through the dark, where I began to imagine recreating a life that actually *felt good* in my body and soul. Instead of one that was written by the stories of my conditioning.

She held me through grief. Grief for every woman in my family who longed to be mothered the way this cabin was mothering me, and for the consequences that rippled through my family because none of us were. Grief for every version of me who tried to be good, when I was already enough.

She made space for my sadness and anger, which poured from every one of my cells as I raged at the systems that demanded my self-sacrifice. The rules that taught me to perform for love. In the years I had lived unaware of these patterns, and the life it had cost me.

The heaviness and depth of these feelings felt like they would never end. But with each release, I saw how they were making room for new experiences with peace and joy.

My sleep deepened.
My eating shifted.
My nervous system unwound from its desperate attachment to proving, striving, pushing.

Even when I returned to my home, the touch of Little Blue Cabin stayed with me. I felt more playful and less serious. My focus shifted from *helping* people to simply *enjoying* them. I connected more deeply to my food, the animals and earth around me... and to seeing the magic in every single moment.

When I would head back for another stay, any tension, fear, or worry would loosen with each mile I drove—and by the time I turned onto the last stretch of dirt roads, my body was soft, my mind quiet, and my heart full of joy.

A joy that made me want to pinch myself every time... *Is this real? Do I really get to have all of this?*

Yes, I do.

Because she called me.
Not with logic.
But with desire.

She pulled me from the depths of shame—the shame of wanting something just for me. Not for my kids, my husband, my parents, God, or my culture. *Just for me.*

At first, I tried to justify our purchasing Little Blue Cabin. I committed to my husband that I would figure out how to pay for her through hosting retreats and putting her on Airbnb. I believed I had to validate the external worth—because saying I wanted Little Blue Cabin *just for me* felt selfish and impractical.

But now, I look back and see how she set me up.
She knew I was afraid to trust myself.

To trust my desires.

I imagine her chuckling to herself like a wise momma knowing her sweet child would someday figure out what she had already learned.

She knew that once I got here, everything would change.

She knew that the moment I saw her on Zillow, dressed in my favorite blue, my heart would skip a beat and my soul would whisper, *What if?*

She knew that after my first visit—when I was certain she was already mine—I would swear my daughter to secrecy. That I would sit for two weeks in silence, wrestling with my shame before finally telling my husband how deeply I wanted her.

Little Blue Cabin was not a good financial investment or a responsible choice by our culture's definitions. She was definitely not the "practical" thing to do with our time and money.

Which is exactly why she called me. And why I had to say yes.

It's been just over a year since we found each other, and the magic has only deepened. The things we have navigated together are beyond anything I could've imagined—both in pain and beauty. I have learned more about myself, and the love, peace, and joy I am here for, than any classroom or pulpit has ever taught me.

Little Blue Cabin shows me every day that Love—God, Goddess, Spirit, Source—holds every part of me. The light and the dark. And has never asked me to change a thing.

It has never required that I earn or perform for it.

Instead, this Love pulls me into Her arms, holds me to Her breast, and sings a lullaby of remembrance: *You are already home.*

Little Blue Cabin gave me a mothering I didn't know I needed. A return to self I didn't know was waiting.

Not a retreat. But a remembrance.
Not a house. But a healing.
Not an escape. But a home.

Trish Leichty (center) + girls

# Dr. Trish Leichty

**Dr. Trish Leichty** is a physician, writer, and nervous system mentor whose work bridges science and soul. With over two decades of experience in medicine and a deep personal journey through trauma, loss, motherhood, and awakening, Trish now serves women who are quietly exhausted from living by the rules—the high-functioning, high-achieving caretakers, helpers, and former "good girls" who are ready to rest, reclaim, and remember who they are beneath it all.

After navigating years of personal trauma—including emotional abuse, spiritual deconstruction, profound grief, and physical burnout—Trish stepped away from the traditional medical path to create a more embodied, holistic approach to healing. Her work now centers on helping women regulate their nervous systems and reconnect with their inner wisdom through breathwork, astrology, energy healing, somatic practices, psilocybin journeys, creativity, and sacred rest.

She is the founder of Beewyld Retreats, intimate nature-based immersions held in the wide quiet of Wyoming, where women are invited into deep restoration and spiritual reconnection.

Trish's work is grounded in medical knowledge and spiritual integrity. She is known for her ability to hold space with deep care and honesty, weaving intuition and evidence-based insight to create experiences that are both transformational and deeply human. Her mission is simple but revolutionary: to help women stop performing and start *being*—with breath, with joy, and with profound self-compassion.

⊕ www.TrishLeichty.com
◎ @trishleichty
Scan QR code to learn more about Dr. Trish Leichty.

# 09

# From Daughter to Mother: A Journey of Discovery and Understanding

*by Melissa A. Ferreira*

Motherhood is more than creating a body for a soul to inhabit, preparing them for the journey of life. This is what I now realize with my own spiritual awakening. You could even say a karmic connection as well, souls coming together for evolution. That is the start. Then we have the experience of watching and caring for this little human, to emerge into the adult, as I have done with my two children. My own journey of motherhood has made me analyze my own experiences each day. This is my reflection.

We carry this beautiful gift in our womb, sharing life force energy, doing all the things we should to maintain health for self and the baby. It brings exciting times of joy and finding love, before we even meet. How can that be? I now understand its connection on a soul level. For me, it was pure joy, love, and gratitude. While sharing those months, we share so much more than we realize. We share our feelings, emotions, stress, and voice. We are one, literally. This is why it is so important to have a healthy attitude and maintain a healthy structure.

As the child grows and we see their personality, we realize what gets passed on to the child. We begin to see ourselves in them, along with our elders. This process is so much more than physical: it's spiritual in nature. As my life develops, I see aspects of my parents and elders reflected in me. Some I'm proud to carry with me, others bring curiosity and require understanding.

As I reflect upon the beginning of my life, I am left with curiosity about the nature of my mother's state of being during her pregnancy with me. I have heard the stories from my mom and other family members, but I sense they are deeper than words can describe. Let me explain.

I am the fourth child in the family. My mother had a couple of miscarriages before my eldest brother was born. She wanted kids immensely and was disappointed after each loss. I can't imagine what that felt like, and she never spoke of it. Eventually, my brother came into this world. Then two years later, another brother. And eleven months later, my sister. I was born four years later and was told it was a "surprise," along with my sister. Mom had a rare blood type, and in the late 1960s, childbirth was very risky for her at the age of thirty-five. Now here she was pregnant again, with three kids, ages seven, five, and four. I can only imagine what that was like; besides being worried about her health, along with this baby she was carrying.

As she carried me through the pregnancy, she told me later that she held feelings of fear, guilt, and confusion, which would be understood. I have realized, through my own healing journey, therapy, and spiritual awakening, that this created questions of my self-worth, passed through the womb. We carry emotions from past generations with us, often creating confusion around our own self-worth, with experiences we don't understand. I eventually came into this world, being the exact duplicate of my mother as well, even down to the fingers. She graced me with her physical appearance, that's for sure.

Mom held the house together well, raising four kids while my dad worked two jobs to support us and give us, just about, all we wanted. We had home-cooked meals, desserts, beautiful holidays, and family gatherings. We had a lake house, where we spent the summers swimming and boating. I'd say we lived a somewhat "normal" middle-class life. Very family-oriented, there was closeness, yet alongside that, there was an underlying darkness that you could feel but not put a finger on. I do believe most couples have love for each other and their family. Back in the seventies, most husbands went to work while the wives stayed home with the kids. I can recall seeing many of the moms around during the day. My mom didn't really have close friends. She was friendly with the neighbors... how close, I'm not sure, as by the time I was old enough to understand, they either moved or started working. I would see my parents going out with relatives and some of their couple friends on the weekends. I was still very young at that time, and from what I can recall, they would mostly go to dinner by themselves or on business dinners.

As with many families, there were moments of dismay between us kids. Arguing over who did what to whom... I recall mom not liking that! That's not fun to see your kids fighting. Mom always strived to have and be the best at everything, even the perfect family, as if she had something to prove. To whom? Herself? Maybe she struggled with self-worth as well. As the years went on, she struggled with depression and addiction to alcohol.

On the surface, everything was wonderful. Looking back, I do recall times where there were signs of dysfunction and struggle, but they did everything they could to not let us kids worry about anything, never speaking of the underlying issues, such as money issues, feelings, or what Mom may have been going through personally.

Even later in life, I never asked about those things. I felt I was the one who really saw the flaws in the family, but I never asked about personal issues. Thinking back, I wasn't really allowed to have that kind of voice. If I tried, I was sent to my room and told I was being disrespectful. So, I learned to avoid and just accept.

Being the youngest, with a gap in age from the others, I spent a lot of time alone with my parents. This was probably why I was more aware of the dynamics of their relationship. We would go for rides, exploring new areas, shops, and have dinner out. I was introduced to quaint little shops, learning the history of antiques, with appreciation, and culture. We always found the best restaurants and tried new food. Something I still appreciate today.

My feelings of low self-worth began to show as I became a teenager. The relationships I had were always superficial. I was what you might consider a "fifth wheel." I was bullied and betrayed, which confirmed my feelings of inadequacy. My school days were a struggle in that regard; I turned to food to heal my wounds, gaining a lot of weight, which led to an eating disorder.

My mom never showed any empathy towards my feelings; she didn't know how. She grew up with an abusive alcoholic father, and my grandmother lived in fear of him. I realize now that she wasn't shown how to give empathy and compassion, as her family lived in survival mode. There's no room for weakness when you are trying to survive; you just push through it. In her eyes, showing empathy represented weakness. She had to have a tough exterior to survive. She lived with fear every day. Expressing feelings wasn't a practice in my family.

Expression equaled weakness and brought an awareness that, maybe, life wasn't "perfect." As I see now, we had to conceal what wasn't perfect. If any evidence showed through the cracks, it was covered up quickly. This, I believe, has led me to my own awareness of the damage that hiding emotions can lead to.

As the older siblings were out or working, I witnessed many nights of dismay between mom and dad. Arguments, possibly about mom's drinking, and not really understanding what was happening, led me to my own conclusions. As the years went on, events like this happened often, but they never let on that anything was wrong between them. I understand now, most parents don't want the kids to worry. These events were never discussed, even as an adult. It goes back to not letting it come out into the light.

As I got involved with high school and work, developing my own life, I shut these moments out. Seeing less meant it didn't affect me. I remember being numb to it all, until one night when I was sixteen years old. Mom and Dad had been arguing, and Mom was drinking. She was in the bathroom, and I had a vision of her passed out on the bathroom floor.

Dad asked me to check on her, and I knew what I would see when I opened the door; my vision had come to fruition. Honestly, I thought she was dead,…until I screamed and she woke up. With the situation at hand, I knew something had to change. I decided to take matters into my own hands and called the hospital for help with her alcoholism. This inquiry never went anywhere due to my father not wanting to bring light to my mom's addiction.

At sixteen years old, I realized I had taken on the role of helper, empath, fixer…just to name a few roles that shaped my life. Destined to be a caregiver to all, even many years later, to my mom in her final month of life. A role I took on then, willingly, without hesitation.

Looking back, I don't regret it one bit—in fact, it was an honor to walk alongside her, guiding her home. Knowing the end of her life here on Earth was coming to an end, which, yes, we both knew, I felt a kinship with her. I had already been involved in the healing modalities, which I believe her soul knew I could help.

After Mom's passing, Dad became dependent on me. I stepped into her role. As I had two children of my own, and being a single mom with a business, it was not an easy task. My heart ached for this man, as he grieved a life he'd known for so many years. I could only imagine how lost he felt.

Mom took her last breath, exactly one year to the date of my divorce. I felt like my childhood was over. When your mom leaves this earthly realm, with her goes the "idea" of childhood. It's as if she carries all the memories… and they seem to die as well. You can no longer ask questions, you can no longer call for guidance, you're on your own now. Mothers seem to hold that knowledge. As the reality of that sank in, all my childhood memories came flooding back. All the trials, trauma, and worry seemed to meld together. It blurred into my thoughts, not being able to make sense of it all. *She's gone now, nothing can change that, acceptance is all that's left.*

I have realized that day wasn't the end of my relationship with that soul I called "Mom", as with my intuition, I have a deeper connection with her soul than I had while she was embodied. Through this connection, I have come to understand so much regarding her experience in this lifetime and how it affects mine. Who I have become in my life, and the mother I am to my children, is intertwined with her essence.

With understanding and compassion, I now honor her journey. I can only hope my children will be able to honor mine, too. My journey of motherhood began when I was twenty-nine years old. After some indecisiveness regarding when I wanted to have kids, I made the choice to move forward with it, probably an unconscious decision when I think back.

My pregnancy was a breeze; I was truly blessed. My son was born two weeks after his due date, with a smooth delivery. It was the most wonderful experience. I had never felt so much joy and love, but at the same time… fear. I was now responsible for this little person, to care for and guide in life's experiences. Seven weeks after his birth, my husband left for the police academy. He was away Monday to Friday, for seven months, leaving me alone to care for our baby, home, and my business.

Even on the weekends when he came home, he was busy studying and trying to spend time with our son. It wasn't easy, as our son was often unwell, especially at night. I was very stressed, and I know he felt it; it's a regret I can't change. When training was done, he returned home to start his new career. With a new baby, a new career, and unsociable hours for my husband to contend with, I was still the main caregiver in the house and held most of the responsibilities.

I would take my son to work with me: all the clients loved him, which I know now, was helpful with his socialization. I loved my life. Even with the stress of responsibility, I was happy. When my husband began to show signs of distance, which I attributed to the stress of his job, we sought counseling, but he wasn't much of a communicator.

Looking back, this was a pattern in my life, which I know I attracted. It was what I grew up with and grew to be comfortable with. In hindsight, the patterns were there from the start. The environment I was raised in taught me to just accept things as they are: "don't rock the boat." The mix of my mom's strong, somewhat cold demeanor and dad's passive behavior, with a touch of warmth, left me confused. I didn't want to give up on my family and questioned if it really was "that bad." I was filled with hope that the nightmare would turn into a dream. Hopeful to have the life I wanted.

I adored my husband at the time, had a beautiful son, and was in a thriving career, as the owner of my business—what else could I want? But there were missing pieces, I felt it in the depths of my soul.

Strength and confidence were not my strong suits, and I was enduring emotional abuse from my husband. Every time I tried to stand up for myself, I was shut down. I began to lose trust in myself, and in him. The lack of loving support left me lonely. My son experienced moments of my frustration, for it was hard to disguise, unlike my parents, who were very good at hiding their emotions. Days, months, and years passed while I adapted to the life I was living, thinking nothing could ever change if *he* wasn't willing to change. (When you are in an abusive relationship, you don't realize it until you wake up!)

Seven years passed, and we discussed having another baby... well, he wanted one. I'm not sure why, as he wasn't really parenting like I was. As I always did... I agreed. I got pregnant right away, so baby number two was on the way. I'll admit I was super excited and again had a fantastic pregnancy. I was older, wiser, and more cautious of my health. With my son, I had gained one hundred pounds, and with my history of an eating disorder, that was always on my mind. I did gain weight and just realized, *I lost it once I can do it again.* I was happy as long as my baby was healthy.

My daughter was born two weeks early due to her cord being wrapped around her neck. The doctor induced me, and within a few hours, she arrived. The most beautiful thing was that I was able to lift her right out of my womb and onto my chest. Talk about instant connection! It was another beautiful moment I will treasure forever.

She had to be in an incubator for a couple of days, which meant I had to be apart from her. When my son was born, he was on the larger side, so I had decided not to breastfeed. With my daughter, I chose to breastfeed, so her being separate was very tough. We eventually went home with this tiny little girl to add to our family. I felt blessed beyond words: two healthy babies, a nice home, money, and our own health. Yet still I felt at a loss.

We went on vacations and did family day trips; the happy little family. A few years later, I discovered my husband had betrayed me. There I was with two young kids, not making enough money to support us; *what do I do?* We again sought counseling and stayed together.

My husband was still working with the police and had become a K-9 officer, deciding to go after a different position and get another dog. We already had a family dog and his prior K-9 service dog. I love dogs, and so do the kids, so we said, "OK." He had to go away again for a few months to train. Another separation: this time, he didn't come home on the weekends.

I worked from home with my business now, which made things a little easier. My son was in school, and I had my daughter home while I worked. I didn't have a ton of help, as family was not available. I had to make the difficult decision to "put down" our family dog, as he became aggressive and was attacking the other dog. He had shown aggression before and even bit my daughter's hand the week prior to my husband going off to training. As he left for three months, I was left to handle everything, my business, the kids, the house, (even during winter), I couldn't add an aggressive dog to the list.

During the time my husband was away, I went to visit him and noticed some odd behavior with one of the women he was training with. This added to my stress of being alone, constantly worrying whether I could trust him. Nothing was ever confirmed, but when you know and trust your gut... You know!

I could see our family was crumbling from the inside, as was I, though we put on a good mask of the happy family for all to see. My love for my children was at the top of my priority list. I prayed every day for things to get better between us; for him to see how blessed we were. My eyes saw a different picture, and I knew I was changing.

I devoted my time to my children, caring for them and being involved with their school and activities. As I look back, I know they didn't have one hundred percent of me. I didn't have it either. It took me a long time to realize this. All the years of suffering, from childhood into my adult life. I was praying for a solution to find myself. I was taking on all the blame for what was going wrong. Thinking I was the common denominator in all the relationships I had, it had to have something to do with me. I did not want my kids to feel this or follow suit.

I realized *I was following the same path as my mom.* I needed to do something, but was always left with threats of no money from him, as well as his gaslighting me. That left me feeling hopeless and stuck. I believed the lies he was telling me about how I couldn't survive without him.

I began to explore holistic healing through a friend. It was just what I needed. This changed my life. I began to find myself, my light, and who I wanted to be. I didn't want my children seeing a stressed-out, angry, and sad mom. No, I was not leaving that legacy for them. I have my ex-husband to thank for that as well. One day, while we were fighting over his "extra activities" outside our marriage, I attempted to take pills to end my suffering. His comment was, "That's a nice legacy to leave your kids." That was all I needed to hear. That was the day I took my power back.

Through my awakening to what was going on in my life, I realized my children deserved more from me. *They deserve a mom who knows her worth. How could I teach them the values of self-worth if I didn't have it?* My healing was the turning point in my life. I did it for myself and my children. We eventually divorced… and I found my soul. My true soul of who I was on the inside. It's amazing what you can "see" when you step out of the grips of trauma. I was blessed to have my family around me more, my friends—old and new—and I thought, *if this was what my life was to be like…that was fine with me!*

As my kids also endured abuse from their dad, they, too, have stepped into true "seeing". I would walk through fire for my kids, and well, I pretty much did. I was fortunate and felt divinely gifted to be freed.

We became the three musketeers. Our freedom gave us many laughs and joyful experiences, without worrying or being fearful if "Dad" would get upset. It wasn't easy, being a single mom with two jobs, trying to bring good things to them. I strived to teach them honesty and open communication, to show love, so they know they are worthy of all of their desires. Sometimes I could see some of their father's behavior coming out in them. When I did it, it became an instant correction, bringing awareness to behaviors that may hurt others. This journey wasn't just about the physical aspects of raising a baby into an adult. It was more about showing them their soul. Teaching them that they mattered and were loved. That all feelings can be expressed, questions can be asked, and honesty would be given. I wanted them to know they were safe… something I didn't truly feel as a child, and for some of their childhood, they didn't either.

My kids are adults now and living their own lives, making their own decisions. Sometimes they consult with me about life, and that makes me feel I've done a good job. They can trust me, and they know what they say matters. I am so proud of the journey we've had together. Though I can't take away their struggles, as I wish I could, what life gives us all serves a purpose of learning. This is something I still teach them.

This experience of being a daughter and then a mother brings so much insight into how the generations work energetically. I have come to see how each one lived. What their beliefs were and how they interact with the next generation. Society carries judgment about how kids should be raised, instilling fear if you don't follow "the rules". That way may have worked in the past; however, times and circumstances change. The "normal" family is, never was, or ever will be "normal." What is "normal" anyway? I can say I didn't follow the "normal" statute; I went with my instincts. Using the tools I was learning along my healing journey. We paved that path together.

My life has been full of joy, love, and learning—and that is what has made me who I am today. The times of challenge weren't easy, yet I survived and thrived because of them. I consider my challenges as blessings to cherish for the experience. I am so proud of who I am, and I know for sure my mom is as well. I wouldn't change one lesson or ask for more of anything. Every relationship I've had has been intertwined for the purpose of the evolution of our soul.

It is a sacred bond between mother and child. As I'm writing this, reflecting on my childhood and my past, I could have written about all the good times to make it a happy story, but that wasn't the reality. Life isn't just a story: it is filled with lessons, and if we don't recognize them for what they are, we lose the ability to hold value in the good times, as well as the bad. We can't go back and change things; we can only "accept." Acceptance can mean so many things, depending on the circumstance. Accepting to feel safe, to keep the peace, accepting to move on, and to learn. If we don't accept, we resist. Resistance persists and keeps us stuck, never allowing us to evolve and grow.

I "accept" full exposure to each lesson, past, present, and future, as I choose growth and alignment for my soul's path of evolution. I give gratitude to my mother for her courage to endure the lessons on her life path, and for sharing them with me on my own path. This is the way I can honor her. This is how each generation shows us how to evolve and break the generational pathway. Each generation passes these lessons on to the next; it's up to us to acknowledge and heal, or repeat. Some generational traumas repeat until someone learns why they were there… understanding, and breaking the chain.

With those lessons, I can assist in the transformation of future generations. I now know that the role of "helper" has taken on a new identity, one I choose with love for all humanity. Turning my pain into purpose brings clarity and understanding to all I encounter. We don't always see or understand why things happen the way they do, but I assure you, one day you will.

I can only hope my children and future generations look back on my life with gratitude and appreciation for the path I have paved for them, for it was done with pure love!

When we heal ourselves, we heal past and future generations. I believe the best gift we can give our children is our healed selves. Leaving a legacy does not have to be so monumental. This is one that may go unnoticed, and I'm ok with that. Sometimes it is the unspoken imprints that make the most impact; they are smart, and they figure things out all on their own. With generational trauma healed, they should go on without that one lesson to endure. Yes, there may be new ones that arise, as each generation will have all new experiences.

I am so proud of the mom I was gifted with, and I am extremely proud of the mom I've become. Being proud of my children is an understatement. They each have qualities meant to leave amazing imprints on those they encounter. I'll selfishly take credit for their huge hearts, desire to learn, and commitment to their own values.

I ask myself often, *If I knew what I know now, would I change anything?*

That answer is a huge **"NO."** How could I? My children are and always will be my life. Not just because I gave birth to them and they are a part of me, but because they are their own unique soul/person. Each day, month, and year, I get to witness their evolution, which makes my heart grow. I will watch and be their biggest fan till I take my last breath. Even beyond that, I will continue to watch over my little angels, just as I know my mom does with me! And if you were wondering...Yes, *I did find the life I always wanted!*

I thank you for reading my story, and hope it touched your heart as much as it did mine while writing it. Sharing our story gives others the comfort to know that they are not alone.

# Melissa A. Ferreira

**Melissa A. Ferreira** is a Soul Body Mentor, Reiki Master/Teacher, Energy Healer, Oracle Card Reader, and Intuitive Coach dedicated to supporting individuals on their journey toward self-awareness and empowerment to transmute old patterns into a new life.

Blending energy work, nervous system regulation, and subconscious repatterning, she guides clients out of survival mode and into a calmer, more aligned way of living—where life begins responding *for* them, not *to* them. With her Light Body Mentoring and Reiki, she connects mind-body awareness to integrate alignment.

Melissa assists individuals in recognizing and reprogramming old belief patterns that may hinder their personal growth. By fostering a connection to their inner authority, soul body, she empowers them to navigate the world with authenticity and confidence. "You don't heal to feel better—you heal to become who you really are."

Melissa creates a safe space for exploration, growth, and transformation, encouraging individuals to trust their intuition and fully embrace their personal journeys. Her mission is to help others cultivate clarity, balance, and empowerment to step out of the old story and into the life that was always meant for them.

🌐 www.EssentialLifeMasteryCoachingHealing.com
📷 @melpeshferreira
Scan QR code to learn more about Melissa A. Ferreira.

# Section III:
# When the Bond Breaks

- Where have I experienced distance or misunderstanding in my relationships?

- What emotions have been hardest to hold or express?

- What might be asking for my attention or care now?

SOME WOUNDS ARE NOT ALWAYS VISIBLE, BUT THEY ARE DEEPLY FELT.

# The Headless Mother

*by Dr. Papa-yoni Das*

I had never placed much stock in astrology. Though I resonate with being an Aquarius, the idea of making life decisions determined, in part, by the placements of planets when I was born, seemed highly imprudent. But, one Peruvian adventure of Ayahuasca-induced insights, followed by my grieving a girlfriend who had left her body soon after my return to the States, created a confluence of circumstances that coaxed me towards exploring the undercurrents of my emotional body. I was called to understand more deeply the makeup and meaning of my life. It was arranged: I would have my Vedic astrologist friend perform a reading.

It was a muggy late August afternoon at his recently acquired home in New Orleans, dubbed Benediction Moon. This mansion turned spiritual sanctuary was a bit of a fixer-upper, so I exchanged some labor for his services. Tuckered out after hours of toil, we took respite before his mandir, where small figures of various Hindu deities dwell. The atmosphere was imbued with the musk of burning sandalwood incense. Wisps of smoke wafted weightlessly, encapsulating us in the moment. I was eager not only to rest, but also because this was the moment set aside for him to tell me about myself. Feigning modesty and surprise, I reveled in elation, hearing him move from one flattering observation to the next. Soon, I would be shaken from my pride as, about a third of the way through, the mood took a sobering turn.

"We come now to your fourth house, wherein resides a headless mother. You have Ketu here. The fourth house rules the mother, childhood, emotional safety, and the feeling of belonging. Ketu here doesn't mean a lack of love, but it does signify detachment—a sense that whatever you needed emotionally couldn't be found in the usual places. And because your moon happens to be in your fourth house as well, the emotional impact this has on you is exacerbated significantly.

"This placement suggests a karmic relationship with the mother: unfinished business, lessons carried across lifetimes, or a bond that teaches through distance rather than comfort. It's the place where effort doesn't bring reward, where attachment slowly breaks down because it's already been exhausted. It can feel like a hollow space —a numbness, a sense that whatever you needed there was never going to come in the way you hoped. People with this placement often grow up feeling like they have to find their sense of home inside themselves, instead of in a family or a place."

"This is spot on, Prabhu," I muttered. I couldn't decide whether to be dumbfounded or depressed. This felt less like the description of an astrological house and more like someone finally naming something I had lived inside for my whole life.

My mother never had the maternal instinct. Not only did she give birth to me at nineteen, but I was her fourth child. I do think that my being her youngest—and her only boy—set me apart to enjoy some modicum of favor. The fact that she still carries my father's last name, even though they've been divorced since I was three, has admittedly given me a sense of connection that my sisters don't have the privilege of claiming. All the same, she didn't raise any of us. I was raised by my father and his parents; her middle two daughters were raised by their father and his parents; and her eldest daughter was raised by my mother's mother.

My mother's relationship to motherhood began long before she was ready for it, shaped by violence and loss in her own adolescence— experiences that stripped her of choice and safety before she ever had the chance to develop a sense of herself. My maternal grandmother, God rest her soul, struggled with her own instability in ways that shaped the whole family. My maternal grandfather abused my mother and her twin sister before abandoning them for another family when they were still children themselves. My mother had the cards stacked against her from the start, and I have always felt sorry for her because of it.

My sympathy extends unbegrudgingly, despite the mental and emotional harm she may have caused me over the years, and there are many instances to consider. One of my earliest memories is of her cheating on my dad. I must have been between one and two years old at the time. She took me with her during a tryst with Andy, the window clerk at our local gas station. I remember being in his apartment, seeing them together on his canopy bed.

I recall another occasion when my mother was holding me in her arms as she ran out of his gas station, just before it exploded! We got out unscathed, moments before the building burned to the ground. I'm not sure whether it was a targeted attack, an insurance scheme, or a random accident… but it must have left some imprint on my toddler's psyche. I'm reminded of that catastrophe whenever I return to my childhood community, where fragments of the structure still sit on a concrete lot, half-swallowed by weeds.

I remember the day my parents separated. My dad had learned of her infidelity and of certain ramifications that couldn't be remedied, so he decided to take me with him. Before we left, he asked if there was anything I wanted to say to my mom.

"She slapped me."

Dad was appalled. My mother vehemently denied it. Imagine that being the thing I chose to say at that moment. I wasn't lying. She had slapped me once after I grabbed her cigarette butts, no doubt an impulsive reaction out of fear that I might poison or burn myself. I had already burned myself once before by pulling her curling iron down from the counter, scars I still carry.

I wonder why my instinct was to inflame the situation further. Why heap more blame onto my mother before leaving? I was likely modeling my father in the moments just prior, telling, in retrospect, of where my sense of alignment lay. I knew emotions were high, but I don't think I understood the finality of what was happening. For years, I carried guilt for my part in that moment.

"It is these sorts of experiences that were written in the stars for you to go through, Prabhu,[1] to mold you into who you are today. Ketu

---

1 Among ISKCON devotees, all males are addressed as "Prabhu". In Sanskrit, Prabhu means "lord" or "master".

shows where you learned too early how to survive without being held. Ketu removes the illusion that something outside of you will finally make you whole. This can feel cruel at first. It can feel like abandonment."

*It all makes so much sense now,* I thought. It explained why she would sometimes make plans with me when I was little and then fail to follow through. I used to cry when she didn't show. Each letdown hurt the same as the last, but over time, I learned not to take her words at face value.

Once, she called to apologize for not picking me up. I told her it was okay, but, after a pause, she asked, "You're not gonna hit me next time you see me, are you?"

The question stunned me. I had never raised a hand to my mother. The thought had never even crossed my mind. I told my grandmother, and she waved an irreverent hand toward the houses down the street and said, "Well, they used to hit your other grandmother over there."

She shook her head, almost amused. "One time she came over asking, 'Am I bleeding?' 'cause one of them done bust her upside the head! So she probably assumed you would treat her like they treated their mother when they were upset."

I never harbored any ill will toward my mother. I carried too much compassion.

Once, I overheard her arguing with her girlfriend at the time. I crept up the stairs and listened outside her bedroom door as she sobbed about having no money. It undid me. Growing up, I never asked her for anything. If anything, I wanted to help her. I wanted to be close to her, to know her. I cherished what little I did know. I'd heard stories about how, as a girl, she used to model, play the saxophone, and earn the best grades. I bragged about her to anyone who would listen—how pretty she was, how talented, how smart.

She's been a blackjack dealer her entire adult life, and I was proud of that, too. I thought it was glamorous. *My mom works in a casino. She can shuffle cards better than anyone.*

As time passed, the illusion wore thin. I began to realize that visiting her usually meant disappointment. When she wasn't at work, she was in bed. To impress her, I cleaned her room, cooked for her, and waited up past midnight until she came home. We would eat together and watch television in bed until she fell asleep. Aside from going out to eat on her day off, that was the extent of our time together.

I came to understand her affection mostly through what she bought me—food, toys, clothes. I let those things cover my dissatisfaction, though not without guilt for feeling it at all. When I was young, her lethargy felt like boredom, something I could work around. As a teenager, it felt alienating, but it also gave me room to express myself freely. As an adult, seeing how she lives feels unbearable.

Her dread is numbed with alcohol and cigarettes. The closest she comes to relief is gambling, which only deepens her despair. What cruel irony it is that she depends on her vice, even enabling others to succumb to it, as her sole source of income. She hates her job, but claims it's all she knows. She's told me she never had a dream for herself, never imagined another life.

It wasn't until I lived with her in Arizona for a few months in 2020 that my sympathy finally shifted—turning inward, toward my own condition.

At the time, my younger boyfriend convinced me that he needed to escape a hostile living situation with his parents. I've always been a protector by nature, and though I didn't yet have a place of my own, the idea appealed to me as a way to help him, while finally accepting an offer my mother had made many times since high school—that I go and live with her.

Izzy and I moved cross-country, from Chicago to Phoenix. It was a full house: my mother, her fiancé, their coworker Jack, and her twin sister were already living there. Still, Izzy and I had our own room, and I was excited to finally live with my mom for more than a month for the first time since I was three.

From time to time, I even managed to get her to read through my metaphysical ministry coursework with me. I felt like I was having a positive influence on her spirit, trying—gently—to encourage a healthier way of living. But the goodwill didn't last long.

One day, while I was driving home from work, my cousin Chris called me.

"Vinnie, just so you know, some shit's been going down at the house," he said. "Izzy and Linda got into it, and she called him a f*ggot."

Linda is Chris's mother. While my own mother is the most depressed person I know, her twin sister is the most spiteful.

As soon as I arrived, I pulled Chris aside and spoke in a low voice.

"You'd better go get your gun," I said, "because if I jump on your mother and you swing on me for it, you're gonna have to shoot me—'cause I'm whooping your ass too, and I don't want it to come to that."

He didn't hesitate. "Shiddd, I'm not gonna stop you."

Linda, Chris, my mom, Jack, and I were all on the back patio. I sat directly across from Linda, a patio table between us.

Very matter-of-fact, I asked, "You called Izzy a f*ggot?"

"He walks around with makeup on, all vain, and can't clean up after himself," she slurred.

"We clean plenty," I said, "but what business is that of yours? That's not your kitchen. This isn't your house. This is my mother's house. If there's a problem, it's her place to bring it up—yet somehow you're always at the center of every problem here."

"I don't have a problem," she said. "A grown-ass man wanting to be a woman but can't wash dishes—that's a problem."

"So you call him a f*ggot," I said, "over some dishes?"

"Yes, I did." She smiled.

"She needs to go."

"We'll see who leaves first. I ain't going nowhere."

"Either you get out, or I'm gonna put you out."

"Ain't nobody putting anybody out," my mother cut in.

I glanced at her, stunned, then fixed my gaze back on Linda.

"I will put your shit out on the street."

"You're not putting her stuff on the street, Vinnie," my mom interjected.

By then, I was burning. Linda and I locked eyes like two animals daring the other to move. Her smirk said everything: *She's on my side. I win.* The longer we stared, the hotter the rage rose in me. I had never felt anger like that before.

Through clenched teeth, I said, "You're a vile, wicked thing."

"Don't say that, Vinnie," my mother implored.

"Shut up!" I shouted, my eyes never leaving her sister. I had never spoken to my mother that way before.

"Think about your spiritual practices," she pleaded. "You're a minister. Remember?"

"Fuck that."

She raised her voice, trying to break my stare. "Look at me. Vinnie, look at me."

I couldn't. If I took my eyes off Linda, I knew where they'd land next—and I didn't want my own mother to become the object of my rage.

"Chris," I said, my voice breaking. "Take me inside. Get me out of here. Please."

He grabbed me and pulled me away. He saved me from myself.

After a brief decompression, my mother and I spoke again. I told her, "If you don't make her leave, then I will go. It's your responsibility as the head of this household to make sure everyone here is safe from harassment or harm. Your sister used a slur. She disrespected your son. To me, the choice is clear."

She begged me to stay. But when it became obvious that I wasn't going to bend, she offered a compromise: that I ask my sister to take me in, back in Indiana.

That was the first time I felt *intentionally* unsupported by my mother. Before then, I could usually explain her failures away—her low self-esteem, her fear, her inability to stand firm. But this was different. This time, she *was* showing up… just not for me. She was choosing against her own interests and mine. Her lack of self-respect had turned into a willingness to let me be disrespected.

That made it personal.

*She couldn't love me,* I thought, *because she doesn't even love herself.*

Izzy and I left within the month.

"That was about two years ago, Prabhu," I said. "Since then, I've come to see that the tenuous relationship I have with my mother isn't contained to her alone. It's shaped how I relate to my entire maternal family—and how I experience intimacy with family, friends, lovers, even strangers."

"In many ways, I've come to understand love *via negativa*—by recognizing what it is not. I grew up with a constant ache for comfort. I learned early how to be alone with my feelings, even when I wasn't physically alone. I learned not to expect too much. The pain wasn't loud. It was subtle, ongoing, and confusing. It lived in my body as a kind of emotional homelessness."

I paused, then said, "But now it's howling, and it hurts. What can I do? How do I fix this?"

"You can try to understand her fallen condition," he said, "as a spirit-soul mired in *maya* and shaped by karmic reactions. But you can't fix her. Your soul isn't meant to find its home through the mother in this lifetime."

Hearing that broke my heart—yet relieved it. It gave me permission to stop waiting for the past to rearrange itself. I could stop asking a wounded person to be my shelter.

The headless mother lingered long after the reading ended. She haunted me, hovering during subsequent interactions with my mother. The next time I saw her—two months later—I could feel it clearly: she was there in form, but absent in presence.

On the drive home, I said aloud, "I don't think I need to see her anymore."

When you begin to cut cords, the people on the other end feel it. In a subconscious attempt to preserve the bond, they make themselves known. My mother started calling me for a change.

At first, I appreciated it. But it didn't take long to notice a pattern and realize she was using me for emotional labor. She'd be drunk, complaining about the chaos her sister was causing and how desperately she wanted her gone. "She'll be gone soon," she'd say. "There are plans to get her out."

Then she would slip into the same familiar script—regrets about her life, followed by the inevitable question: "Do you think your dad loved me?"

I was willing to listen at first. I wanted to be there for her. But eventually it became clear that nothing I said was landing. My reassurance and encouragement passed straight through her. Each conversation replayed the last, almost verbatim, until the repetition began to feel unhinged.

"I feel like I can say these things to you," she'd tell me, "because I always thought you were my wisest kid."

One day, before she could get started, I stopped her. "You keep calling me about the same things you're not willing to change," I said. "I want you to live a more fulfilling life, but I can't want that more than you do. I'm sorry—but don't call me anymore unless you have something good to talk about."

"Okay, Vinnie," she said quietly.

"I love you," I told her.

"I love you too, Vinnie," she said, and began to cry.

We hung up.

My heart still breaks when I think about it. She has rarely called since.

I thought I had healed enough to stay with her for a while during a tour out west in 2025. Her sister was still there, but I told myself I could let bygones be bygones.

Linda didn't just revert to her bullying ways—this time, the harassment crossed into something more sinister. She made snide remarks. "You're a heathen," she sneered. "My son is better than you." She provoked me deliberately, baiting me, hoping I'd strike her so she could have me arrested. Were such a scenario to transpire, I had no reason to believe that my mother would come to my defense.

I texted my mom. She replied, "I'm sorry about Linda. She's not gonna be here too much longer. That's already in the plans."

I tried to endure it. To ignore her. But eventually, I refused to subject myself to any more abuse.

"I thought I'd let you know that her harassment today included following me around and jeering, 'I got the best of you. You're finally leaving. She's my sister.' And that sums it up. She takes pride in you enabling her at the expense of others. You've chosen her again, and you've done so by abandoning your responsibility to protect me. I'm going to show you how to cut cords with someone who causes more harm than healing. That's the only gift I have left to offer you."

"She'll be gone soon—I told you. I love you very much. I know I haven't been there. I am weak. I want to do better. You'll see. I just didn't want her to be homeless. I'm starting to accept that might happen. Please don't give up on me."

That was exactly what I was doing. I was giving up—not in anger, but in clarity. I intended to wash my hands of her completely and never return.

On the day I was leaving, my heart was heavy. I had rehearsed many times how I would say my final goodbyes. I hugged her—long and firm.

"Take care of yourself. I love you," I said, with an emphasis meant to last a lifetime.

Tears welled in my eyes as I stepped back, trying to take in as much of her as I could before my vision blurred and the dam broke. I turned and headed for the door.

"What's wrong, Vinnie?" she called after me.

Without turning back, I said, "I gotta go," steadying the quiver in my voice.

I ran to my car, sat in the driver's seat, and bawled. I stayed there for several minutes before my mother came outside and saw me. She asked me to come back in and talk with her before I left.

I hate to see her cry, but that final heart-to-heart gave us a gentler send-off.

I have tried for years to make it make sense, how she could truly love me as she claims. I settled on the explanation that she said it simply because it was expected. *She doesn't really love me,* I told myself, *but she probably doesn't know that she doesn't—and that's okay.*

I lived with that conclusion until a different understanding emerged.

I now believe that my mother and I share a complicated soul contract. And before we entered these bodies, I imagine myself asking her—spirit to spirit—for something extraordinary.

*I want you to be my mother in this life,* I might have said, *but you are emotionally unavailable.*

I imagine her recoiling at first. *I could never do that. I love you too much.*

And I imagine myself answering, *In an infiniverse of love, what greater gift than to experience its absence? What deeper growth than learning to generate it from within?*

Perhaps she agreed—not because it was easy, but because it was necessary. Because love, in its most radical form, sometimes looks like deprivation. Like sacrifice. Like choosing a role that wounds in order to teach.

It would hurt her to hurt me. And it would hurt me to know that. But maybe we both consented to the pain, trusting it would expand us in ways comfort never could.

If that is love, then perhaps I have known it all along.

Through all I've endured, I've learned how to pan out and see love through a wider scope. It requires reframing and a surrender of my ideas about what love is supposed to look like.

Healing the mother-wound isn't about blame, but grief. Grieving the version of mothering you needed but didn't receive. Grieving the child who learned to self-contain too early. Grieving the quiet loneliness that followed you into adulthood. It's about walking through grief without closure, knowing it may never fully disappear. We're asked to carry the mother-wound consciously, without letting it define our worth. And slowly—patiently—to learn how to give ourselves the safety we kept searching for outside of us. When that happens, the ache doesn't vanish—but it stops running your life. The longing for nurture doesn't disappear; it transforms. Over time, the wound of not feeling fully held becomes wisdom, discernment, empathy, depth—and the ability to sit with pain without being destroyed by it, to hold space for others without losing oneself.

That doesn't mean I've erased her from my life. It means I've stopped asking her to be something she cannot be. I still speak to her. I still love her. But I meet her now as she is, not as the mother I needed or wanted her to be. The relationship remains—but no longer as a place I go looking for home.

Papa-yoni Das (right) and his Mom

# Dr. Papa-yoni Das

**Dr. Papa-yoni Das** is a spiritual practitioner, writer, and ritual artist whose work centers on trauma integration, shadow work, and the cultivation of spiritual maturity. He is the founder of AzaZealous Outreach, a ministry devoted to spiritual education, healing, and the reclamation of inner sovereignty through lived experience rather than dogma.

Through AzaZealous Outreach, Papa-yoni offers spiritual counseling and tarot readings, and creates energetically charged devotional tools designed to support personal transformation. These include Inner Child Necklaces, crafted to aid in trauma healing and integration, and Kundalini Keys, a series of sacred adornments aligned with the chakra system and embodied awakening.

He is also the guiding force behind the Temple of the Peacock Flame, a contemporary mystery school dedicated to reverence, self-knowledge, and the disciplined exploration of spiritual truth. Blending personal narrative with esoteric insight, Papa-yoni's work invites others to meet their wounds with honesty, compassion, and courage—learning to build an inner home where one was once absent.

🌐 www.AzaZealousOutreach.com

📷 @azazealot

Scan QR code to learn more about Papa-yoni Das.

# 11

# Sacred Fury

*by Tracee Dunblazier*

Deep in the night, around 2 am, a little seven-year-old girl urgently tossed and turned in bed, hoping for sleep to come soon. Riddled with anxiety and the fear of creatures that would be sure to arrive along with the night terrors that always did, the incessant rolling back and forth seemed to be the only thing that would soothe her weary spirit. House rules dictated that she could only play her music until 8 pm, so the rest of the night she was on her own, through the nightly solo journey into the hell that awakened as the sun set.

Every morning was the same. As I walked into the kitchen for breakfast, my mother would ask, "Tracee, what on earth happens to your hair at night?"

The bob-styled haircut, ruffled around my face, but the entire back of my hair was matted and sticking up, like it had been caught in a dryer.

"Nothing, Mom, I just wake up like this."

Ever since I can remember, and all through my life, I reveled in each sunset and sunrise. Basking in the golden hour brought a much-needed sense of stability and peace that would wash away as the Sun dropped behind the mountains. The nightly demonic visitors would come. Sometimes in the form of dreams with the inevitable chase, assault, or murder from some forgotten time. Standing up in the crib, crying in the middle of the night, waiting for the darkness to lift, was my first remembering of the beginning… of what exactly, I did not know.

No one in my home had hurt me. From all accounts, looking at the outside and even the inside view, we were a joyous, happy family. All was right with the world… except for me, as the night fell. There was no conflict between my mother and me; we seemed to be born with a sound respect for one another, although the adolescent years were a bit of a struggle. After dad died, I was the only one (youngest of three) who seemed to notice my mother's pain. Many times, I would catch her crying alone in her room, and I would go in to offer her comfort: comfort she seemed grateful for and uncomfortable with all at the same time.

I was twelve years old, and the art of grief hadn't been discovered in my family; it was the stoicism that was trustworthy. In retrospect, the bond I shared with my mother was long before its time; like a lightweight, fire-resistant carbon fiber composite that would one day house a drone. You couldn't tell how strong our relationship was because the connection it housed was so light and airy, you could barely feel it. Nonetheless, as time would tell, it was the weight of the karma we each carried with us, and the ghosts that roamed the lands, that would reveal the true nature of our alliance.

For me, the hauntings were continual, and as I got older, I began to understand the silent weight of trauma my mother and father each sustained. Having been born around the Great Depression and growing up in the backdrop of two world wars, the lessons were clear:

How you felt wasn't going to feed the pigs or put food on the table.

Sharing your feelings was dangerous.

Time always reveals the divinity of our human emotions and how they cast a wide net, reaching from our ancestors to their descendants, on all levels of energy over time and space. All the unexpressed devastation, looking for a time and place to tell its story. The silence can become thick with it.

Yet, like the spirit of water, nothing is more potent than the relationship of a mother to a daughter, and from a daughter to herself. The relentlessness of deep passion is the most penetrating pain. While somewhere in between those is the least spoken of—clearing a space for light to dwell. It's not very "lady-like," therefore, it is relegated to the dark midnight hours, sometimes revealed only in shame-filled sobs. It is the sacred power of divine fury. Its vibration seeks the darkest corners in which to destroy illusion and forge a path to the truth.

Why are the ladies so mad, you ask? Women have been endowed with the responsibility to access a profound depth of the soul. A place where only mastering one's rage can divulge the true essence of its mystical power. Over the millennia, we need only to look at cultural gender roles and the human struggle for the greatest delusion to be conquered: dominance.

The simplest expression of this is the age-old parasitic dynamic of a patriarchal system seeking to stifle the power of women. The subtle indoctrinations of a society patterned to make a woman feel powerless and worthless, suitable for only certain tasks, or submissive to men in general. And encouraging men to suppress their own access to the divine. Phrases like "boys will be boys", "man up", "be the man of the house," or "act like a lady" are only a few of the ways we train men and women to diminish themselves and stifle their divine essence.

The household I grew up in in the sixties was, by all accounts, deeply conservative. Dad had a big job in the media and didn't want my mother to pursue a career. They agreed on having two children, but ended up with a third: me. My father got his start in radio fighting in the Korean War. Both of my parents left their childhood homes by the age of sixteen and forged lives for themselves where they could. My father enlisted in the American Air Force, and my mother shared a studio apartment with a roommate (at the time, called a "bachelor's" apartment, no doubt because it was odd or even inappropriate to see a woman living on her own). She supported herself by working at the local bank.

Neither left their families with the excitement of starting a life on their own. Rather, it was a murky launch from the bitter clutches of confusion and fear, with violent undertones. Not surprisingly, they found one another in their early twenties, and life began anew for their muddled partnership. They had so many connection points and things in common. My father, Tom, was profoundly funny with an unsurpassed dry wit, and my mother loved to laugh. Audrey was a singer, and Tom loved music. They both grew up in emotionally erratic households with their opposite-gendered parent expressing some form of what was considered, at the time, "mental illness."

During the Great Depression, America struggled with its deeper feelings, too. It was a generation tasked with managing truthfulness, farsighted and critical thinking, all while beginning to discuss and understand the human psyche. However, the inevitable drive for dominance was a key factor in the collective unconscious of the patriarchy, governing all those who sought to discover how the mind works and ways of healing "erratic behavior" or "intensity", often seen in those who expressed a broader spectrum of emotion, or experienced the multi-dimensionality of consciousness. (Mostly in women or young men.)

At the time, the need for "healing" was really a collective patriarchal desire to diminish a misunderstood force that could not be contained or controlled in another. The Frontal Lobotomy, a procedure to cut out a portion of the brain to direct emotional expression, was created in 1935 and disproportionately given to women to manage anything from schizophrenia to depression. These operations often left their victims devastated, with deep emotional and cognitive deficits.

Who is to say where these wounds we carry begin or end, as we only need to look to our collective history to see the echoing patterns of growth, confusion, frustration, and violence as they reverberate through time. We become witnesses to how our systems of communications, religion, or governance use their influence to indoctrinate a society into the values that subtly exclude and denigrate specific members.

## My Mother's Name Was Rage, My Name Was Grief

Who knew that my mother and I would meet again at the intersection of time and space. I, too, left my childhood home directly after high school, almost to the day. I was excited to live on my own, sharing an apartment with a workmate. Shortly thereafter, the ignition of my karmic rage was lit, from suffering a sexual assault. From my very core, I knew my mother would not be able to help me. I knew the emotions that were beginning to fire from deep within me meant help was beyond anything or anyone I knew. I also understood that the depth of what was beginning to emerge would be misunderstood by Western ways of thinking about the psyche. What I needed existed somewhere else, and I needed to find it *immediately.* Emotional Intelligence and empathy weren't yet "causes" in the 80s, and deep spiritual trauma was only spoken about by a few. The vivid suffering I'd always felt during my night-frights had usually released themselves with a mixture of prayer and tears. But now, there was a new game in town: fury… and it seemed vaguely familiar.

My mother and I had many things in common: we both loved to sing, cook, craft, and create a beautiful home. I got my looks from my mother, and we both loved make-up and fashion. Both of us never quite felt safe, ever, which made it hard to resist the impulse to make abusive people feel comfortable in their behavior by being "nice". It was only time and experiences that would reveal the feelings of rage we had in common.

As a child, conflict resolution was absent in the home, and my mother and I found ourselves alone. During my teenage years, she would rage, I would cry, and someone would leave the room. It's true that two equal forces cannot exist in the same space. There was no room for my hidden rage, while hers was so blatant. I cried. Both of us, no doubt, were fueled by hormones—but make no mistake, they are not the reason for your feelings—they just ensure the revelation of their meanings.

I don't suppose I can truly have an honest discourse on the ancient rage passed down to me (the liberating fires sabered by my grief), without acknowledging the mirrors to my primordial story. Medusa: a woman abandoned twice in her first few months of life, laid bare on the temple steps for the goddess Athena to find. Medusa was grateful and loyal to Athena and took great care to be of service in the temple. After many attempts by Poseidon to engage with Medusa, her rebuffing each one, he raped her. As the myth was later interpreted and then translated from its original Greek, Athena (the virgin Goddess), so infuriated at the desecration of her temple, blamed Medusa for the sexual assault she suffered, as if she'd had a choice and was somehow disloyal. Athena blamed the victim and cursed Medusa into a snake-haired creature who could turn people into stone. She was eventually murdered by Perseus.

How many of us wince at the realistic telling of the story? How often do we soften the edges of our pain for the sake of others? It's no wonder women find themselves continually frustrated, fragmented, and enraged. It only takes a history lesson to point it out.

It took me decades to understand that my mother and I were made of the same stuff for different reasons, and our struggle was to see ourselves in each other—good and bad. I could see her, and she could see me… and it was devastating. Neither of us had the skills, at the time, to stay in the room and work it out. It became my mission to garner the tools to request, reveal, accept, and express the many layers of rage that lay beneath all I did and felt.

The answers were everywhere, from literature to social mores; the stifling of our Starseed, from which we access our power, was prevalent. For hundreds of years, male editors have changed the true meanings intended by righteous authors, not only in pieces like The Odyssey, but in many other texts, like ancient myths and religious books.

They imbued the literature with their bias. Editor Emily Wilson's version of The Odyssey[1] notably translates controversial terms like "handmaidens" as "slaves," highlighting social hierarchies that other translations have shrouded with polite euphemisms or victim-blaming. Interestingly, as in the case of Medusa, women were only given the illusion of power to make men seem righteous and measured, or to obfuscate their bad male behavior. Wilson makes a powerful point: "The Odyssey traces deep male fears about female power, and it shows the terrible damage done to women, and perhaps also to men, by the androcentric social structures that keep us silent and constrained."[2]

Emily Wilson is the first woman to publish a complete modern English verse translation of Homer's Odyssey—it changed everything—and the response was profound. With over a million ratings on Goodreads, what was all the frenzy about? For the first time in more than three millennia, a woman had translated what Homer's Greek text was directly saying, even though it made the story much more uncomfortable to read.

---

1 Published by W. W. Norton & Company, 2018
2 *A Translator's Reckoning With the Women of the Odyssey*, By Emily Wilson. *The New Yorker*, December 8, 2017

My mother and I shared many hidden traits. We shared a deep integrity and moral compass, not by obligation, but by choice; decisions that were forged from surviving something powerful. My mother's silence towards me was the way she could honor the revelation that I became for our family. She had a deep impulse to make others feel at ease, while I was driven to recognize and communicate the truth, no matter how vulnerable we all felt. My mother was the keeper of the secret I was born to express. My sacred pattern was to reveal the truth in a way that could be shared, received, and celebrated, even in grief. This was the way I honored my mother.

Reconciliation of these deep karmic wounds, in the years my mother and I spent together, struggled. For years, I characterized it as, "I cried, she yelled." It wasn't until I began to more fully understand the lens she experienced life through, the one shaped, in part, by bouts of flaring paternal rage and yawning maternal stoicism. All these things, no doubt, are rife with misunderstanding from the indoctrination of the unrealistic and confused gender role models of the 40s and 50s. To be clear, my characterization isn't from a judgment of the choices of others; it is a reference to the generations of "traditional" roles being molded from misappropriated fear of feminine power, cultural needs based in survival, and misinterpreted metaphors and human archetypes served up in centuries of male-dominated media and literature. The issue isn't the expression of these ways; it is the portrayal that they are a tradition, which implies we should all express ourselves in this way if we hope to survive.

Almost twenty years after my mother's death, I came upon a box while cleaning out my attic. It was filled with items belonging to Audrey during her teenage years and early twenties. In it, I found newspaper clippings of my mother and her three-girl group winning talent shows with their version of Boogie Woogie Bugle Boy. There was a scrapbook made of construction paper, complete with the smell of time, and the frayed edges of dashed dreams. It was clearly her version of a vision board with magazine cutouts of lipstick colors and couture fashion. She'd written affirmations of places she'd one day go to, and work she'd do.

Of course, the vision board came true within the options available to her. She was one of the most fashionable and elegant women I've ever known, who loved makeup and always wore a lipstick-color to match her outfit and fingernails. My father was a regional celebrity, and they traveled many times to beautiful places near and far. However, she was *not allowed* to work or sing professionally during her marriage to my father.

I am certain, after going through my mother's youthful effects, that she was modern before her time. She may have made different decisions or reveled in the opportunity to express herself in a very different way, had she not been guided by the fear of reprisal or an obligation to the values of a society that held limited expectations of her—had it been an option.

I suppose this is the riddle of any life: figuring out the mystery of finding joy in the limitations set forth for us by our circumstances. My mother and I were made of the same stuff, indelibly linked—I was the tip of the iceberg, she was the base. Two powerful, yet opposite energies, are going through life being forced to see themselves through each other. The first time I experienced the sacred rage we both carried, I began to understand what had, as of yet, only been conflict between us.

We were arguing about something, I don't remember what, but I was sixteen and felt deeply misunderstood. She and I were facing one another in the corner of the kitchen when, in her frustration, she took her open hand and smacked my arm. Time seemed to stop. I felt a force of purpose and presence that rose up in me: I don't know where it came from, other than that it dwelled deep inside me. I looked her in the eye, and with my open hand, hit her arm in the same place with the same intensity. I felt her rage well up, as we were locked in that moment.

All I can say is, moments later, the ferocity with which we met one another, dropped. I don't have a solid recollection of what happened next, probably I cried, but what we both learned that day, from one another, is that we were meant to be allies, never enemies. At the time, I didn't understand the pain my mother carried, in addition to being widowed, but as I said, she was the base of the iceberg.

The one thing I always appreciated about her was her limitations regarding me. I knew she loved me, but the best she could do was to trust me to take care of myself, take my own counsel, and share the wisdom I was born with, as it occasionally stumbled out.

Luckily, I was happy to have such curiosity about perspective versus reality. I wanted to unravel all the profound emotions I experienced and to answer the deeper questions in life. I wanted to understand the patterns and traumas that plagued my family, the world, and myself. I was grateful that my grief gave mercy to the conflict born from the harder truths of my spiritual heritage. By the time I was in my late twenties, I'd found a way to resolve the profound emotional divide between my mother and me, but it was not until my late thirties that our relationship could truly express its purpose.

Audrey received a diagnosis of lung cancer, and somehow, I was not surprised. Over the previous two years, I had had a series of dreams, visions, and interactions with my mother from the ethers. She was letting me know that something was coming. She had been visiting for my sister's fortieth birthday party, and as the designated driver on our car ride home, I turned to see my mother's brother, Lee, with his arm around her in the back seat. Lee had been dead for years. He didn't say anything; he just held her in a comforting way.

A few days later, we were winding down a big friends and family dinner at a local Mexican restaurant where the margaritas were flowing. Mom and I were sitting next to one another and giggling about something when the expression on her face turned serious. She said,

"Tracee, you're going to have to take care of me."

I replied with a laugh, "Don't you want your favorite daughter to take care of you?" A joke I'd often made with her about my sister.

"No," she said. "You will have to take care of me."

*Hmmm,* I thought. "Okay, Mom, yes, of course, I will take care of you."

Once again, she relaxed into the social celebration, but I was never the same. That night stuck with me for months, until winter came, bringing her diagnosis with it. Now, I was clear on her meaning. This was her time, not to overcome the cancer but to surrender to the transition to a world in which her power could be expressed fully. Her mind didn't know it yet, but everything about her demeanor revealed that this was the time to make amends with anything left unfinished in this world, and I was to be her guide.

Up until this point, no one quite understood or knew what to do with what I did for a living, but this circumstance was finally bringing a little clarity. My mother and I began communicating in a way we never had. Sometimes across the table, sometimes by phone, but mostly telepathically. In all the years of her second marriage, she had never disparaged her husband or made mention of any rift in their relationship, but spending time with her in that nine-month journey revealed a lot.

He was an alcoholic who often threw temper tantrums when he didn't get his way. His daily ritual was to pour a twenty-ounce whiskey and water by noon so that by early evening, he would find something to be belligerent about—on several occasions, he got angry at her for "divorcing" him. This was how he processed his grief for her dying and leaving him behind.

One evening, I'd been staying in my old bedroom in their home. I was on the phone with a client when he burst into the room, exclaiming that my mother needed me. I ended the call and rushed out to the den, where we had her hospital bed set up. As I walked through the kitchen, he was there waiting for me, yelling at me as I walked by. In one quiet movement in passing, I raised my finger, looked him in the eye, and whispered, "No," while I kept moving to the den to see my mother.

As it turns out, she only wanted to know where I was, so I sat down in the easy chair near the doorway to watch some television with her. Wayne, who had been stewing in the kitchen, finally barreled into the doorway just behind me, again, screeching with anger because I wouldn't participate in his tantrum.

This time, turning my body in the chair to look up at him, I looked him in the eye, and in a deeper and more resonant voice, I enunciated, "You will not speak to me in this manner." I turned my head back around to see my mother focused straight ahead, petting Pearl, the little white kitten the neighbors would bring over to visit, her body reduced by the cancer, her hair slightly growing back. She was chuckling with a look of glee on her face. Wayne was standing behind me, frustrated and confused, and as his fire was going out, he made one last self-pitying remark and left the room.

In those two minutes, I began to glean what my mother had been going through; the divide in their relationship and the loneliness she'd been feeling, never once speaking of it. The look on her face was poetic in its triumph; someone had spoken up for her, someone had stopped the bully. I soon came to feel that all the struggle of being who I was in the world had given me a set of skills that fully prepared me to be with my mother in her final days.

Until recently, I had never considered that I was a feminist. I didn't understand the box society had put me in because I see the equality and righteousness in all people, no matter what. It didn't occur to me that when friends said to me consistently, "you just need to find the right man", that the undertone was pointing to my inability to compromise in ways women were just expected to, still. I didn't know what that was.

I now see that my mother's silence offered me a blindness to the expected female submission to male dominance. It was the most powerful gift my mother could have given me. She loved me in the most influential way she could—by giving me freedom. She refused to indoctrinate me in the social mores and traditions in which she was steeped, but instead offered me the opportunity to unreservedly express who I was born to be.

Tracee Dunblazier and her Mom

# Tracee Dunblazier

**Tracee Dunblazier GC-C** is a Los Angeles-based spiritual empath, shaman, and 68-time international award-winning author and publisher at GTP. As a multi-sensitive, Tracee's blend of intuitive information, combined with different modalities, has provided the opportunity for thousands to achieve deep healing and cultivate the success and peace they seek in their lives. Tracee enjoys podcasting and speaking internationally on mind, body, spirit topics. As President of the Coalition of Visionary Resources, the trade organization for the Mind, Body, Spirit marketplace, Tracee manages the COVR Visionary Awards program and educational opportunities for MBS businesses. Her latest published works: *Oracle of the InBetween 48 Cards & Guidebook, Transformative Grief: An Ancient Ritual of Healing for Modern Times*, and *Your Crystal Allies Book and Card Deck series*.

⊕ www.TraceeDunblazier.com
ⓕ www.facebook.com/TraceeDunblazier
Scan QR code to learn more about Tracee Dunblazier.

# 12

# A Miracle of Forgiveness

*by Jan Casebolt*

*This chapter includes sensitive material related to suicide, mental health struggles, and a parent attempting to harm their child. These experiences are shared as part of a journey of healing and transformation. While the story ultimately moves toward understanding, healing, and forgiveness, some moments may feel intense or activating.*

I remember the first time my Mom tried to kill me. I was twelve years old and had just returned home from school. Mom said she wanted to go for a ride in our Volkswagen Van. It was my favorite car. We bought it brand new off the lot. It was a beautiful blue and white color, and the interior smelled of new vinyl. My Mom was an amazing artist, and she had painted a pink moustache, a purple mole, and big eyelashes on the front of the van. She named it Kether and, as it was 1975, was one of the first to get a personalized license plate. We loved riding around in Kether. People smiled, honked, and waved when we drove by.

My two younger brothers hopped in Kether, and I put my baby sister in her car seat. I took my usual, coveted spot in the front seat, next to Mom. As the eldest child, I had many responsibilities, but one of the perks was "dibs" on the front seat. This would prove fortuitous on this particular drive. We drove up the hill past my friend's homes to the top of our neighborhood. Mom drove off the paved street onto a dirt road where four-wheelers often drove. "What are you doing?" I asked. "Let's have a little fun," she said with a slight smile. "Mom," I said in my most parental-sounding voice, "I don't think Kether was made for off-roading." She laughed and pushed her foot down on the gas pedal. My brothers screamed a little, and we slid a bit on the dirt road. We bumped around, which made her laugh harder. Not a fun kind of laugh you might hear during a comedy movie or the giggle of a friend, but an eerie-sounding laugh that gave me instant chills. "Mom, stop!" I yelled. "Stop right now!" She didn't listen. She picked up speed. My brothers were fully screaming, and we were heading for a drop-off near a turn on the dirt road. "Mom," I screamed to no avail. "Stop! There's a cliff!" Her laughter increased, and I remember feeling terrified as the drop off loomed ahead. "Help us, God!" I yelled. I reached over and grabbed the wheel, turning it just in time to avoid going over the edge. It was a split second, yet it felt like a million years. "Stop!" I yelled again, and this time my mother listened.

She stopped the car and pulled on the emergency brake. We sat there in silence for one long minute, then she crumpled over the steering wheel and sobbed. I didn't skip a beat. "What the hell is wrong with you?" I yelled. "Take us home… now!" Her sobbing subsided, and the look in her eyes changed. She drove us home in silence. The air felt heavy, and I broke the silence in the same way I had grown up watching my Dad do it. I started yelling at her. "What the hell is wrong with you, Barbara?" I demanded. "We have a baby in the car! We could have been killed!" It would be many years later, in counseling, that I would come to terms with the fact that it may have actually been her plan. We pulled back into the driveway, and Mom disappeared into the house. My brothers climbed out quietly, and I got my baby sister out of her car seat. I scrounged up some food, found a bottle for the baby, and took care of business. *Someone has to do it…!* I told myself.

The second time my Mom tried to kill me felt like a scary movie.

I needed something for the baby, and Mom wasn't in her room. I searched from room to room calling her name and finally heard a noise in the garage. Our garage had boxes from our recent move, and our large dining table and other furniture were inside. I found my Mom sitting in front of her old vanity. She was staring at her face in the mirror, pulling on her cheeks, as if to tear them off, and crying.

"Mom," I yelled. "What are you doing?" But she did not respond; she just kept staring, pulling, and crying, then started hitting herself in the face. "Mom! Mom! It's me, Jan! Mom?" I tried to get her attention, when suddenly, she grabbed the mirror and threw it on the ground. It made a horrible, crashing sound and shattered into several large pieces. "Mom!" I ran over to her in horror, yet she still did not see me standing there. She bent down and carefully picked up one of the shards. It was shaped like a dagger. She finally looked in my direction… but she did not look like herself. Her eyes were squinted, and her face was drawn up into an unnatural grimace.

She snarled, "Get away from me!" raising her arm and the shard of glass. She lunged in my direction. I screamed, and this made her laugh. She came towards me, taking lumbering steps with her long legs. I quickly ran around the old dining table. She chased me around twice before I bolted for the door. I made it just in time, quickly locking her in the garage. She pounded on the door. "Open this door!" she demanded, her voice sounding very different than normal. "No! No way. You can stay there," I yelled. The adrenaline coursed through me, and I was breathing heavily as I started to tremble. I was always effective in a moment of crisis, but the aftereffects would sometimes catch up with me.

My baby sister started to fuss in her crib, so I snapped out of my fear. I left Mom locked in the garage and went to check on my sister. After an hour or so, I put my ear to the garage door. Mom was gently tapping, and her voice sounded normal again. "Jan? Jan? I'm sorry. Can I come in?" she said.

In a perfect world, I would have had adult support as I held my hand on that garage door handle. I would have had someone to make the decision for me and ensure we were safe. But that was not the case. Our nearest relative, my maternal grandmother, lived two hours away. She was busy with her job at El Toro Marine Base and her many social pursuits. When I tried to call her for help, she said, "Jan, you're just a child. I am sure you're exaggerating. I'll come down at the end of the month." So there I was, with my hand on the cold garage doorknob, feeling sorry for my Mom crying on the other side, yet scared for my own safety.

"Are you sure you're OK now?" I asked her. "Yes. I'm tired. I need to feed the baby." She got to me with the baby care statement, and her voice did sound normal. I slowly turned the knob, alert and ready to run. I opened the door and backed away. I held my breath as she emerged, but recognized her face again as she stepped into the house. There were tear stains on her cheeks and a few red marks, but the grimace was gone. She stepped past me quietly as if nothing had happened.

Things weren't always like this with my mother. The memories I hold dear are the fun and carefree times. My mom was very artistic and loved music and books. She spent long hours reading everything from Shakesphere to Dr. Seuss while I sat happily on her lap. My love of writing, music, and poetry is directly connected to her. She was incredibly intuitive and psychic. She would always know when things were about to happen. "Jan, answer the phone. Grandma Mary is calling," she would say just moments before the phone rang. She would tell me to go open the front door, just before the doorbell rang. When I began to see spirits and "things that weren't there," she was loving and helped me to understand it. When my dad was at work, she was lots of fun. We would turn the living room into a giant fort. We had newspaper ball fights and made elaborate art projects. We baked cookies and made fudge.

One of my favorite memories is helping her stir the brownie batter and her letting me lick the spoon. The smell of brownies baking reminds me of her and always makes me smile. She let me brush her long, brown hair, and I thought she was the most beautiful woman on Earth. I wanted to be just like her. She was kind and courteous: I observed her putting the needs of others first on many occasions. When an elderly woman locked her keys in her car, Mom gave her a ride home to get a spare. If someone needed a hand at the grocery store, she was right there to assist. She taught me that respecting our elders and being kind to people was very important.

She also loved being a mom. When my younger siblings were born, she explained the changes in her body in the most positive way. She taught me that being pregnant and having a baby was a special, sacred gift. She let me place my hand on her belly when my younger siblings moved in her womb. She never complained during pregnancy and seemed to glow. She taught me that breastfeeding was best and that caring for a baby was fun.

Because of her positive influence, I always wanted to be a mom. There are photos of me as a toddler holding two baby dolls, one in each arm. I took my "babies" with me everywhere—into the sandbox, the stroller, and into bed with me. My brother was born when I was two-and-a-half, and was placed into my arms. I was taught how to care for him. I played with him, read to him, learned how to change his diaper, and fed him.

Caretaking came naturally to me, in part because I was hypervigilant. As a spiritually sensitive and intuitive child, my parents' marriage taught me to walk on eggshells from my very first steps. My father was a successful and intelligent civil engineer who liked things organized. He was often frustrated with my relaxed, artistic mother. I learned to read the signs of an impending argument and worked hard to cheer up my father as "his favorite." As time went on, I would often step in front of my mother during a fight… so she would not be hit. It baffled me when my mom allowed herself to be disrespected at home, since she was beloved everywhere else.

Over time, my own disrespect for her crept in, beginning when I was five years old. I remember being swept away to a neighbor's house late one night, while my mom went to the hospital. My siblings and I came home the next day, and Mom had a black eye and stitches on her lip. I was furious. Her beautiful face was marred, and her soft brown eyes looked defeated. "Why?' I asked her, with all the indignation I could muster. "Why didn't you hit Dad back?" "I couldn't," she said, "I love him." "That's dumb!" I yelled. "He hit you!" And I stomped off to my room.

This would begin a shift in my relationship with my mom. She would often say something that did not make sense to me. I would rally against it, be reprimanded, and learn to stuff my feelings. My sense of self became overshadowed by caretaking and "being good" as a way to survive. If I could make my father happy at dinner, he might not get mad at Mom. If I could keep my siblings and me occupied and quiet, we might not get pulled into a fight. I still dreamt of being a mother myself someday and vowed I would "do it better." I told myself I would never let any man hit me, and I would be the best mom I could be.

I did not yet understand that my father was an alcoholic… and my mother an empath without spiritual protection. I was too young to realize that childhood subconscious programming has a way of repeating itself, unless we dig out the tap root of trauma and release non-beneficial belief systems.

As time went on, my parents moved us around quite a bit. They liked to buy homes, fix them up, and sell them for a profit. During my early childhood, we bought a mansion, an orange grove, and a 3-acre fix-er-upper in Vista, California. I loved moving, as I got to choose my new room and decorate it with my mom. She became very bright and cheerful when we did anything creative. The Vista house needed more work than my parents had bargained for, and it became a source of stress and horrible fights. My mom started hanging out with my teenage babysitters while my dad was at work. It was the 1970s, and we went to strange stores where black lights shone on posters, and things smelled "funny." I scolded her when she took us there. "I don't think we should be in here, Mom. This is not a good place for kids," I would say. She would laugh at me in front of her friends and tell me to relax, but that was not possible. I knew we would get home too late to properly clean the house before Dad came home, and the nighttime would become hell.

One particular day, after a horrible fight, my dad went to work and never came home. I called my mom a liar when she told me he'd had a heart attack and died. We had an Irish wake, and my Mom was the perfect hostess. There was alcohol and dancing and many toasts to my dad. My mom never cried: she was stoic the entire time.

I was much too young to understand the complexities of her emotions, but I was old enough to recognize her rapid decline. She sank into a depression and stopped cleaning the house. She stopped taking my siblings and me to school unless I begged her. She spent more time with our teenage babysitters, drinking and doing drugs. Then she met a young Marine. He came to stay with us for a while, and my mom became pregnant. She perked up and was excited to bring a new life into the world. Determined to make things work, she did not want to tell her young boyfriend. He was leaving for special military training the following week. She put her own feelings and needs on hold and decided to go it alone. She moved us to a smaller home in nearby San Marcos, just before my sister was born. I was thrilled to help with infant care again. The only problem was that Mom started sleeping all the time and relying on me more and more. She began behaving strangely and stopped functioning. I would grow to understand that the years of verbal and physical abuse, the lack of support, as well as psychedelic drugs, from the "weird shops," had taken their toll.

Importantly, her intuition was still sharp, but she had no spiritual practice to protect her. She started reading spell books and drawing funny diagrams on the windows. Soon after that, our doors started opening and closing on their own, and I had the horrible feeling of being watched each night when I went to my room. I started sleeping with the light on and praying as hard as I could to God to protect me. My favorite aunt had taught me that I had a guardian angel and that God was always with me. That knowledge has been my compass for as long as I can remember.

A few days after Mom chased me with the shard of glass in the garage, a life-altering event happened. When I came home from sixth grade, the house was especially messy. My mom had been going through boxes. My baby sister was crying, and Mom was on the couch. I took on my father's role and yelled at her about the messy house. I demanded she feed the baby as I started scrubbing the kitchen floor. Midway through the scrubbing, she came to me. "Jan," she pleaded, "Please put the floor scrubber down. Let's go to the park and have some fun together today." "We can't," I said. "The house is a mess, and we have no food! How can we have fun?" I picked up the scrubber again while she stared at me. Her eyes were full of tears, and I saw an unforgettable look of despair. She stared at me for a long time, then simply walked away.

Moments later, my youngest brother came running in. "Jan! I think Mom is hurt!" He was seven years old and looked very worried. I dropped the floor scrubber and ran into her bedroom. Her long legs were sprawled out on the carpet in the bathroom, her head lying on the tile floor next to the toilet. She was making a horrible gurgling sound as she choked on her own blood, and blood was spilling out of a huge hole on the top of her head. "Go get the neighbors…" I yelled to my brother. I dropped to my knees and grabbed my mom's hands.

She had folded them perfectly across her chest, and a gun with a silencer was lying beside her head. "Mom. It's going to be OK. I love you. I'm sorry," was all I could say. I repeated it like a mantra.

The neighbor's oldest child, a sixteen-year-old boy, came in. He saw me holding my mom's hands, saw the gunshot wound and the blood, and gasped. "Call 911," I yelled. I waited with my mother until the ambulance came. The ambulance drivers arrived; I could see shock in their eyes. I can only imagine the scene–a twelve-year-old child sitting with her mother while the life force drained out of her skull. I explained in terms well beyond my twelve years what I thought had happened. One of the ambulance drivers threw up, just as the police arrived.

I tried to convince them I should stay with her, but they told me they would "take it from here." I grabbed my sleeping baby sister, her diaper bag, and a bottle, and went across the street with my two brothers. Thank God for the neighbors taking us in. I watched from the window as my mom was wheeled out on a stretcher, a halo of bloody bandages wrapped around her head. She was pronounced dead that afternoon.

My siblings and I spent the night at the neighbors', waiting for our grandmother to arrive. That night, Mom's spirit came to see me. I felt her walking toward me down the hall. I covered my head. She came very close, and I felt her presence next to my bed. "I am sorry, Jan, I love you," she tried to say. But I wasn't hearing it. "No! Get away…" I was very upset. I could feel her remorse, yet had no space to take it in. I was in shock, upset, and not ready to forgive.

My brothers and I would spend one year with my grandma, and four years in a foster care situation. My baby sister would be adopted by a family that could not have children of their own. My heart was broken, held together by the need to survive, though I continued to be the "carer" and "being good." No one would talk about my mother or the suicide. I stuffed my grief and anger away, doing my best to navigate an abusive foster home, while a deep feeling of abandonment and loneliness crept in. I relied on my belief in God and my guardian angel to keep going. I viewed my mom as weak, and that made me want to be stronger. I always chose to remember the good things about Mom. Her beauty, her kindness to strangers, her love of books, art, and nature. I ignored the fact that she was a victim of domestic violence; an unprotected empath, stifling her own feelings and needs. I stifled my own emotions while trying to move forward: of course, dragging both of our pain into my own adult life.

At eighteen, I ended up moving to Hawaii after taking a trip for high school graduation. The natural beauty of the Islands and the warm welcome of the people sang to my soul. I instantly felt at home and at peace. In Hawaii, I wasn't an orphan or an unwanted foster child; I was a smart, pretty young woman filled with hope.

I attended the University of Hawaii and wrote for the school newspaper. I hiked, surfed, connected with great friends… and I healed. I read Louise Hay's *You Can Heal Your Life* and began to understand that my mom did the best she could with the tools she had been given. I read John Bradshaw's *The Family* to understand the dynamics of my childhood roles. I attended Inner Child workshops and learned to give myself what others had not. I completed a Bible College program and became a youth group leader and lay pastor. I volunteered with local charities and worked for a social service agency. EMDR counseling helped to take the sting out of the memory of finding my mother's body, and I thought my healing was complete.

I would come to understand that healing and evolving are a life-long process, occurring in divine time.

I became pregnant and was thrilled. I took child psychology classes, joined parenting groups, and took care of myself physically. I used the rest of my inheritance from my father to stay at home for as long as I could, and, like my Mother, I found growing a new life inside of me to be a sacred experience. My second son was born four years later, and I was overjoyed. Two step-children entered my life, and I felt incredibly blessed. Having children of my own and being a mom continues to be one of my greatest blessings. But it also made me aware that my own mother left me to fend for myself. Repressed anger and emotions I had stuffed in hidden places began seeping into my heart, and resentment festered there.

When my sons were teenagers, we moved back to where my life began, Long Beach, California. Both my mother and I were born in Long Beach, and I ended up living around the corner from where she grew up. It became even harder to stifle my memories and feelings regarding her untimely death. I pictured her as a beautiful teenager, swimming the canals of Naples Island, training for the Olympic swimming team. I envisioned her painting and going to school. I found myself in my own alcoholic marriage, and realized I had subconsciously repeated the empath/narcissist pattern I observed in my youth.

Unlike my mother, I would not stand quietly and cry during injustice and abuse. I would rally and fight back. The stress and the strain took a toll on my immune system, and a cosmic set-up occurred. I became sick with an "incurable" autoimmune disorder called Sarcoidosis. I have observed that, often, autoimmune disease begins in the fertile soil of childhood trauma, repressed emotions, and non-beneficial beliefs. The body can only hold this energy for so long, and microorganisms find their way in to create the dis-ease.

I spent three long years in bed. My alcoholic and narcissistic partner was unable to put his personal needs on hold, so I relied on my children and hired help to physically care for me. My feelings of abandonment returned with a vengeance.

Modern medicine did not have an answer or cure for Sarcoidosis, so I turned to my faith for help. I prayed every day for a miracle, spending hours listening to spiritual meditations. I became determined to heal and took my personal inventory. I journaled and asked for forgiveness for my own parental shortcomings, asking God to remove the resentments in my heart. One day, I listened to a Subconscious Repair meditation for many hours straight. It was a powerful process and very purifying.

I had a huge realization about my mother: I had a moment where I literally felt her pain. I understood how her sensitivity and nervous system were overloaded through years of emotional neglect and physical abuse. I felt her loneliness and feeling of unworthiness. I realized she died of a broken heart, and ending her life was a symptom of spiritual need, deep pain, and emotional suffering. Tears streamed down my face as a wave of compassion washed over me.

I remembered the episode in the garage and how she didn't look like herself, understanding how the abuse, sadness, and spiritual vulnerability had infected her. I realized she had given me the great gift of knowing the importance of spiritual protection and connection to the divine, and that setting boundaries and healing emotions was integral to personal peace. The mom I knew and loved would never want to hurt me. I felt my anger melt away and fell asleep feeling great empathy and love for her.

I had one of those dreams that felt *very real.* I dreamed I saw my mom. She was young and beautiful and full of light, walking near a stream, picking flowers. She saw me standing there watching her, and she came toward me. "Jan, I love you. I never meant to hurt you. Please forgive me," she said. "I do forgive you, Mom. I love you!" And then, something beautiful happened. She looked up to the sky. My grandmother, who had died two years earlier, reached out her hand and pulled my mother upwards. They floated into the clouds and disappeared in a stream of light. I felt peace wash over me as tears flowed down my cheeks. I woke up as the stream of light was fading on my ceiling. I was sitting up in bed, with real tears on my cheeks. I felt different. I knew in my heart that my forgiveness had finally set both of us free.

Two weeks after forgiving my mom, I was led to a workshop with a clairvoyant, spiritual teacher named Master John Douglas, known for helping autoimmune disorders and mysterious afflictions. He identified two unknown bacteria causing my Sarcoidosis and, through his spiritual insight, used directed prayer to cure me *instantly.*

I was overjoyed! After three years of horrible pain, I felt the powerful frequency of God run through my body; I danced around the room in gratitude. I obtained laboratory tests with clear inflammation markers to prove what I already knew: forgiving my mother had opened my heart, allowing for a miracle to occur.

It has been over a decade since forgiveness and a physical miracle changed my life. When I think of my mother now, I feel peace and love. The sacred bond of motherhood can be beautiful and serene. It can also be incredibly messy. It can smell like brownies baking in the oven, or look like a river of blood on the floor. It can shatter our hearts like broken glass or nurture our evolution from beyond the veil of death. It can grow us, stretch us, and soothe us, depending on what our soul came here to learn. And it can create a cosmic set-up for a miracle to occur.

Thank you, Barbara, my ever beautiful mom. I love you.

Jan (right) with Justin and Adam

# Jan Casebolt

**Jan Casebolt** is a survivor of suicide and the "incurable" disease Sarcoidosis. Her passion is sharing the good news that miracles are possible and supporting others in finding their way to perfect health. She is a mother, writer, and prayer facilitator. She holds a Bible College degree and has 35 years of lay pastor experience. She is a graduate of the Elite Development Course through the Global SELF Foundation and believes that unearthing the tap root of childhood trauma and healing non-beneficial belief systems supports lasting, positive change.

⊕ www.JanCasebolt.com
◎ @JanCasebolt119
Scan QR code to learn more about Jan Casebolt.

# 13

# From Grief to Gratitude

*by Maria Mahboubi*

"I don't ever want to see you again, not even on my deathbed."

Those final words on the page echoed in my mind for years. They were the last things my mother said to me after I consciously chose to estrange myself from her, again. It was clear I had hurt her and myself. The thought of never seeing her again haunted me as the days, weeks, and years went by. It was one of the hardest decisions I've ever made, but it was the one that finally set me free.

I believe we choose our parents before we're born. I believe I chose my mother because some part of me knew she would be my greatest teacher. Our relationship has been difficult, yes, but it has taught me more than any other and has consistently held up a mirror to my inner work. From a very young age, I understood how different we were. To gain her recognition, I had to set myself aside and become who she needed me to be. That pattern became the work of my lifetime.

I became an introvert, a loner, and deeply connected to what I call my *existential grief*. I was born with a sense of profound loss and an ache for the world and all living beings. It was my constant companion ever since I can remember. My mother became inseparable from the existential ache I could not escape. This was my destiny—my mother's love, her rejection, her betrayal. I saw it all as one inseparable truth, woven into the fabric of our story together. The harder she tried to *make me* understand her, the more I shut down and pushed back. And that became our dance.

When I became a mother, something shifted. I understood her more clearly, yet felt more bewildered than ever. I had created my own life, full of love, meaning, and responsibility, and our relationship was no longer just about me feeling motherless—it affected everything. Her actions struck harder. Her words cut deeper. She was my child's grandmother, and I held onto hope that things could change. Unfortunately, they didn't. As she continued to be herself, I became more critical, more vulnerable, and more protective at the same time. My actions were calculated and led by fear; I became more rigid and less forgiving.

As I struggled with how things "should be," I found myself going down the rabbit hole of self-pity… and that took over my life. It occupied every thought, permeating through every cell of my body. I retreated into the familiar grief that was safe and "justified." I claimed that I was alone and had to "do it all" by myself. I didn't need her physical help, I was always very independent and self-sufficient. What I yearned for was the moral support of knowing she was there—unconditionally. This lack created such a deep void inside me that I could no longer ignore it.

Gradually, I recognized I'd made "grief" a part of my identity. As legitimate as my pain was, it had become a way to rationalize my beliefs and behavior. Clinging to that grief, and the identity it created, kept me stuck in an unbearable cycle of feeling like an outsider, like a victim. I condemned her patterns, but I was repeating them in my own way—through suffering and hiding, rather than rage.

As the years went by, I understood her better… though accepting that understanding was another matter. I held genuine admiration for her strength, her resilience, her unwavering fortitude, but those weren't the qualities of a mother who could just be soft with me, who could simply hold me, which is what I truly longed for.

She became a beautiful grandmother to my three children, and I felt deep gratitude for the light she brought into their lives. When she was with them, her own little girl would emerge—full of magic and innocence. I longed to see that version of her more often. I wished desperately we could have met in that tender space, both of us guided by our wide-eyed, uncynical inner children. Something deep within me whispered that we'd been there together before, perhaps in another lifetime. It felt achingly familiar, blessedly safe. But those moments came so rarely that I couldn't hold onto them for long. So I kept our relationship in my head instead of my heart. I understood why—I was protecting myself from more pain. And she was doing the same.

My mother's childhood was difficult (though that's an understatement). She had no choice but to grow up fast, and she did so with impressive resilience. She learned about responsibility and hard work from a very young age; she understood that the skills she had were the only way to survive. And she did survive, in unimaginable ways. She believed vulnerability was weakness, that being unguarded meant being destroyed—and she would resist both, no matter the cost... even if the cost was us.

I worked tirelessly to be different. To silently demonstrate that my way of living actually worked. I saw myself as softer, gentler, someone who led with her heart rather than her wounds. And in many ways, that was true. But I was also in denial. Deep down, grief was steering me—the grief of feeling like a motherless child for so long, the grief of my past, the grief that had become inseparable from my story. I wasn't only living from my wounds, I was parenting from them too!

The realization hit me hard. Because the one job I pride myself on is showing up every day and doing my best at being a parent. Raising emotionally healthy children is what matters most to me. That might be one of the many blessings of having a mother wound: you try harder. Your definition of motherhood becomes central to your actions and your choices as a parent. In 2020, these choices were soon to be challenged when my oldest child developed a life-threatening eating disorder. My first reaction was one of complete and utter despair. I let myself be swallowed by grief, and it felt safe. It took me two weeks to rise up and take massive action. But, through this process, I noticed a pattern. And I questioned it... maybe for the first time.

Grief had shaped my sense of self for so long, and I had been its willing architect. So, there I was, asking:

*How often had I let grief take the lead?*
*How much power had I given it?*
*How much was I attached to it?*
*How could I separate myself from it?*

My relationship with my mother was a reminder of the grief that I carried, but it was not the cause. I cannot blame her for something that has always been inside me. In order for me to overcome it and transform it, I needed to stop resisting it. Because as much as I understood and surrendered to it being a part of me, I had let it control me and shape my decisions, too.

As I stood there in front of the immense challenge of saving my daughter's life, I also took stock of all that really mattered in life. The list was smaller than I expected. As I was faced with a very clear choice, I was finally able to separate myself from the claws of my familiar grief. It was then that I discovered my inner strength and resilience, which I had not previously given a chance to flourish. All of a sudden, everything falls into place when your purpose is bigger than you. And that consciousness shift creates a new reality. Her survival and recovery were all that mattered, and I knew that grief had no place if I was fighting for her life!

During those two-and-a-half years, I made a genuine commitment to transform. I had to be present—not only for myself but for my family. They deserved me whole, without the walls I'd built, ready to take that final step and finish what I'd started.

After years of healing and growth, I was finally willing to release my hold on pain. That recognition became the gateway to a deeper journey: learning to sit with my grief, to truly know it, so I could one day let it go.

When it came to my grief about my mother, I stopped fighting with myself, and my grief turned into profound sorrow, as I recognized that certain needs would never be met. I understood that not all wounds can be healed, and some losses are permanent, even while the person is still alive. My grief taught me to accept that it is ok to continue to parent myself as I parent my children. It taught me that I don't need to feel it as a constant emptiness; instead, I can embrace it and allow it to shape me into a new version of myself.

So, this time, as I let my mother go, I genuinely let myself go as well. I let go of the attachment to how I thought things *should be*. I let go of my expectations of her as a mother and of myself as a daughter. I let go of the guilt. I let go of the story. I knew I had to finally surrender and feel it all.

As I made the decision to fully grieve, I turned to my ego, faced it head-on, and surrendered. At this point, I had nothing more to lose. I had lost my mother. I had to live with that reality, so I gave myself time to fully mourn her loss. But this time, it was from a place of acceptance, not self-pity. I went deeply into my process, which was painfully transformative. I acknowledged who I had been and who I was ready to be *now*.

So I chose. I was given clarity about the path I'd taken and the reasons behind it. I saw the ancestral grief living in me, understood where it came from, and why I'd held onto it.

Beyond that, I experienced something overwhelming: the collective pain of humanity reverberating through every cell. Feeling it was excruciating. Resisting it made everything worse. I understood I had to stop fighting and allow myself to surrender. And I did. It wasn't dramatic. There was no buildup or revelation. It was understated, almost ordinary—it just was. The change emerged through faithful trust, through asking the creator to lead me, to compassionately show me my complete truth, so I could step into full authenticity.

When the sun finally rose inside my soul, the lightness of simply "being" took my breath away. I felt weightless, as if walking on air. The world looked the same, yet everything was new. New and still. Something dormant inside me had awakened—the truth of what had always been available. It confirmed what I'd somehow always known: life was happening for me, never to me. This was rebirth. Suddenly, with startling clarity, I understood that all of it—my story, my suffering, the identity I'd constructed around grief—had purpose. Transformation only required that I lean into it rather than resist. The possibility flooded through me: *I could live without carrying this weight.*

That's when I tasted real freedom, the kind that comes from releasing self-created chains. My mother's wound was genuine, but I had a choice to let it define me or refine me. In that moment of clarity, I finally saw her—truly saw her. Her beauty. Her pain. Her hard-won wisdom. I accepted all of it. Whether she'd healed from our separation didn't matter anymore… though I hoped she had. What mattered was my own healing, my transformation, my ability to shift perspective and embrace her exactly as she was.

In the end, my grief became my greatest gift. It allowed me to truly know my mother and gave us a chance to start afresh. The relationship isn't perfect, but it's honest. Real in a way it never was before. Now I can offer her a love she had never before experienced from me—not because it wasn't there all along, but because I'd been unconsciously reinforcing her narrative of loss and betrayal. That story may still live in her, but I'm no longer feeding it. I can see her soul now and meet her with my own; fully present and unafraid.

Life will never stop presenting challenges. I've come to understand that the real work isn't avoiding difficulty—it's staying open to who I'm becoming through the lessons each challenge offers. My personal evolution is ongoing. Blind spots will always appear because the ego is intrinsic to being human. Yet I've discovered that anything is truly possible. I once resigned myself to never being close to my mother, convinced that gift wasn't meant for me in this lifetime. Now I know with certainty that whatever unfolds in my life is mine to work with, and mine to transform into what my soul yearns for.

So yes, the seemingly impossible is possible. Sadness can shift into joy, obstacles into opportunities, grief into profound gratitude. I have so much gratitude for the lessons; for the way grief sheltered me, for how it accompanied me through the years, and eventually delivered me to a sense of belonging. The alchemy of grief into gratitude has been the most surprising revelation of my life. In releasing my grief, I found not only myself but also my dear mother.

Maria Mahboubi (right) and her Mom

# Maria Mahboubi

**Maria Mahboubi** is a somatic wellness practitioner whose work centers on helping people reconnect with their bodies to release stress, emotional tension, and chronic holding patterns. Through coaching and practices like breathwork, meditation, and somatic body-based techniques, she helps clients tune into their bodies, process their limiting beliefs and emotional wounds, and find a deeper sense of ease and presence. She aims to help people *take the load off*—so they can move through life in an embodied way with more clarity, resilience, and freedom. Ultimately, her goal is to empower people so they can make more awakened and aligned choices. She hosts monthly workshops called "Somatic Wellness Evenings", holds breathwork and meditation experiences, and sees clients 1:1.

Maria lives in Los Angeles with her husband, three children, and two fur babies.

🌐 www.theAwakenedChoice.com
📷 @theawakenedchoice
Scan QR code to learn more about Maria Mahboubi.

# 14

# The Love We Learned

*by Nancy D. O'Reilly, PsyD*

I will begin at my beginning.

According to my parents, I came into the world a scrawny and hairless three-pounder, quite fragile and very small. I spent the first few weeks of my life in an incubator, unable to keep formula down…there were worries I might not make it. I was called the ultimate volcano, and projectile vomiting is not a pretty sight. After trying different formulas, they realized cow's milk was my food of choice, and once that happened, I began to grow. Through it all, my father, a patient and kind man, came each day to the hospital to visit me. He later told me he never doubted my future when he saw me kicking and screaming inside that small, enclosed container. I can picture him now—standing there, cheering me on, quietly urging me to survive.

I assume my mother was absent during those early days because she had a two-year-old daughter at home to care for. My big sister, Stephany, would later become my companion and, at times, my worst enemy. There were no pictures of me until I was around six months old. I can only imagine my parents were worried about whether I would come home at all.

You may be wondering where my mother comes into this story. I was told that when she went into the hospital, the nurses remarked that she didn't even look pregnant. I have often imagined myself in her womb, saying, "YES, I AM HERE!" I have also wondered whether my mother feared I would not survive, and how that fear may have shaped our closeness. Our relationship did not begin with what would be called "bonding."

As I grew, I became focused on learning how fast and how far I could go. I would leave home early, taking the family dog with me on my adventures. I was told I was not an easy child, and that my sister was "perfect." We were often dressed alike for pictures and events, made to look like twins. As a result, I wore the same dress for four years. This became a family ritual—one I would later repeat with the first of my three daughters.

Being dressed as a twin, I had to find *me*. People talk about second-born children wanting to be different, and that became my mantra. I grew up finding ways to do my own thing.

Looking back, I think bonding was a problem for my mother.

I was the child who sucked her thumb—often while running as fast as I could, thumb tucked firmly in my mouth. This became an issue. Stopping me from "embarrassing" the family seemed to become my parents' focus, or at least that's how it felt to me. The hunt to break the habit began. They tried hot sauce, soap, a doctor's kit, and finally, an English racing bike. I managed to suck my thumb through all of it—except the bike. You can't ride fast and suck your thumb at the same time.

What a great idea. My drive to go fast—and to distance myself—only increased. There is nothing like the wind in your hair when riding a bike. That bike took me places, and the urge to drive or ride any mode of transportation became my biggest thrill. I was even able to get a tractor going at a very early age. I was determined to keep moving.

My mother was a very busy person. She became a top real estate agent and was involved in many civic organizations. She was concerned about her place in society. She had grown up in an abundant household and was considered a beauty. From her, I learned what I came to call the "gift of gab." I would watch her on the telephone, listening as she talked business. She even had a box phone, long before cell phones existed, which, at the time, felt pretty amazing.

Children watch, listen, and feel what is going on around them. Looking back, I can see how my mother's upbringing shaped her relationship with love and intimacy. Her family dynamics helped explain a lot of what was missing between us.

Her mother, Mama Nancy, was a 4'11" spitfire who made up for her small stature with a sharp tongue and an oversized personality.

She ran the family business, selling beautiful jewelry, china, and crystal, while my grandfather's love was gambling and playing the stock market, which meant he was often busy doing other things. My grandfather was the larger-than-life showman, while my grandmother was the serious, determined taskmaster.

My mother and her mother had a difficult relationship, marked by struggle instead of closeness. My grandfather favored my mother, and that favoritism created conflict between them. Mothers and daughters can compete for a father's or husband's attention and love, something I came to understand more clearly as I grew closer to my grandmother. My mother often used her relationship with her flamboyant father to get what she wanted. She was the center of her father's world, while my grandmother watched them from the sidelines. I was told that before my grandfather died, he called out for my mother and not for his wife.

That dynamic did not create a loving bond between my mother and grandmother. I did not believe my mother loved in the way I imagined "most" mothers do. I told myself I would not allow this pattern to continue in my own family.

I don't remember my mother hugging me or showing much affection. Her attention was focused on my appearance and my behavior: be nice, be pretty, don't suck your thumb...and don't disagree. I think this only made me more determined to do the opposite, creating even more distance between us.

Once, my mother told me, "I'm surprised you turned out as well as you did." This was the way I was mothered—by a woman who had spent much of her life competing for love and attention. It was not a good lesson to learn.

My father was a different kind of parent. He was a hardworking aviation professional and an accomplished musician. When he wasn't working, he was either playing in an orchestra or flying his plane. He built and flew airplanes, and his love for flying was evident—he lived for that time each day. He was a good father and wanted the best for me. He told me to work hard in school and "stay out of trouble." It was good advice, but it was not my plan. I wanted freedom—to grab life and live it with all the energy I could manage. *Where would that lead me?*

His parents were very different from my mother's. My grandfather was an attorney who felt called to the Methodist ministry. My grandmother was a gentle, kind, soft-spoken partner who supported him fully in that decision. Together, they devoted their lives to service and worked to create one of the first retirement communities in the Midwest, built on the belief that people deserved dignity, care, and peace at every stage of life. I grew up visiting the residents, listening to their stories, and sharing in their personal treasures. As my own children grew, I took them along, too, making those visits part of our family life.

Those memories remain among my fondest. They offered me an early model of partnership, purpose, and quiet compassion—a sharp contrast to what I saw on my mother's side of the family. My parents, with their night-and-day backgrounds, came together and built a family. My mother was outgoing and loved attention, while my father was more serious—dedicated to his work and his calling as a Gideon.

As I grew, I knew I was different than both of my parents. I wanted to be free—independent, with purpose and distinction. Being a wife or a mother was never part of my early plan. I didn't date many boys in school. Instead, I worked and made my own money, so I could get what I wanted without asking for it. The more self-sufficient I became, the more I liked it.

My independence created a distance that became my protection: both from my parents' constant disapproval and from the fear of feeling abandoned. I avoided closeness and relationships to maintain that protection, rejecting others before they could reject me. I also became a tomboy. I played sports and played with boys. Boys didn't come to my house to date me—they came because they wanted me on their team. I could kick a ball as far as most boys and was learning how to compete and survive in my own way.

Fast forward to college. I still had no long-lasting relationships, and that was exactly my plan. We're told that God has plans for each of us before we are born—plans we've somehow signed up for. By then, I had forgotten whatever I might have agreed to, and I was firmly against any plan that included marriage or a baby carriage.

*Where was I headed?* I transferred my sophomore year to a small Midwestern college—one where my parents had significant influence, which they used to help me get accepted and enrolled to attend. I had spent my high school years working and making money, and that did not include earning good grades. I was sent to a small, middle-of-nowhere town and an even smaller college to begin what was supposed to be *my new life.* To say I was unhappy would be an understatement.

The school revolved around sororities and fraternities. So, to fit in, I rushed and became a sorority girl—but that meant more rules, and now, multiple girls were telling me what to do. That was truly horrible. One of our required duties was attending sorority and fraternity exchanges. We dressed up and went to the houses to "meet the boys." And that's where I met my first, and only, love.

I was completely off balance, confused by my feelings, uncertain about what my life would be. For the first time, I was in love… or at least experiencing some powerful chemical attraction.

Love, marriage, and the baby carriage were expected to follow a familiar order. It did not work that way for me. Instead, it was love, then baby, and then a wake-up call. I had no plans to be a mother and was terrified by the news—terrified by what it meant and of what others would think of me.

The man I loved wanted marriage. I wanted to run away.

My family and his family wanted a marriage...and still, I wanted to run away.

I didn't stand much of a chance. The majority won, and the marriage took place.

I was a junior in college and had not yet graduated. I was deeply sad about that. I had become a psychology major, and more than anything, I wanted my degree. I share this because it offers a clue as to where I was headed after marriage and the baby carriage. Psychology would become my muse and, ultimately, my saving grace.

I married at four months pregnant. My mother's comment still rings in my ears: "Thank goodness you don't look pregnant!"

And just like that, we were off to Disneyland.

Five months later, I delivered my daughter, after being heavily drugged, with no memory of giving birth. I was told I used very colorful language during the delivery. Later, they brought her into my room—a seven-pound, six-ounce baby girl. She did not look the way I had imagined. She was a girl. I was a tomboy, and to me, girls were weak and silly.

My relationship with myself as a woman was not favorable. And now, I had given birth to one.

After my daughter's birth, I went back to school, worked, and did my best to be a married woman with a child. I don't remember much of those early days. What followed was the birth of more daughters and the earning of three more degrees. My survival became tied to producing results. Each degree raised my confidence and my resilience as a wife and a mother.

After my second daughter was born, I lost a baby. At the time, I was working on my master's degree in counseling, and I felt like a failure. I believed I had lost that baby because "I had no business being a mother." I felt like I was being punished. I often said, "God… she has a really big sense of humor, giving me daughter after daughter to get my attention."

Slowly, I came to terms with the fact that being a woman was a gift, and realized I needed to treasure what I'd been given. My last daughter came into my life as that gift, though I didn't recognize it until later. She was born without drugs or the interventions I had experienced with my other two daughters. I was able to see her moments after birth… and I saw her smile at me.

It was a joy I cannot fully describe—a deep peace I had never known before. For the first time, I felt what I imagine many mothers feel when they see and hold their newborn. During labor, long before ultrasounds could reveal a baby's gender, I was asked what I wanted. I had listened to her heartbeat for months and knew from its quick rhythm that she was a girl. When asked, I answered proudly and loudly, "a girl." In that moment, I finally took ownership of being the mother of my baby girl.

With her, I was given a chance to love her and, finally, to love myself. I am not saying it changed my life overnight, but it opened a door and allowed me to see what I'd been missing.

I adored my children, but did I really take the time to love them: to hold them, to be close, and to truly enjoy them? Looking back now, I can see both what I achieved and what I missed. I had told myself I would be a better mother than my own mother had been. She once told me she wished she had been closer, and I found myself saying the same thing to my three daughters.

My daughters are grown now and have blessed me with grandchildren and great-grandchildren. I have seven granddaughters, one grandson, and two great-grandsons. I am truly blessed, and continue to learn from each and every one of them.

I have apologized to my daughters for not always being the loving, caring mother they deserved. Sadly, I had not learned, or been taught, how to be one. I now understand that my own mother did not receive those lessons either. I forgave her long ago.

I once promised myself I would be different, yet in many ways I followed in her footsteps, repeating what she did or did not give. It has taken time, but I am learning to *forgive myself.* Each day, I choose to reach out, to love my children and their children more fully. I see that my daughters have learned to love in ways I was not always able to do. Learning never stops.

From my relationship with my own mother, I have realized that forgiveness is not a single act, but a journey. Despite my hopes for my daughters, I see now that forgiveness is part of their lives too, just as it was part of mine. It is a road worth walking, and the words in this chapter are part of that journey.

In fact, my youngest daughter, Ragan Thomson, and I have taken on this book project together, each contributing a chapter as part of our shared process of reflection and healing. We have learned and grown alongside one another, and we continue to share our stories, not only here but also through events and other writings.

Love is imperfect at times—shaped by experience, misunderstanding, and forgiveness—but as it grows, it reveals a depth of beauty and blessing that cannot be rushed. If I have learned anything, it is this: grace matters. For ourselves, and just as much for those we love.

To all of the mothers, or the someday or soon-to-be mothers, please know this:

Each day is about loving yourself and forgiving yourself for what you did not yet have the words, ideas, or knowledge to understand. We all start with blank pages, and over time, we fill them with love and lived experiences as mothers. Love yourself and love your children more. In the end, things have a way of always working out.

Dr. Nancy O'Reilly
with her daughter Ragan Thomson

# Nancy D. O'Reilly, PsyD

**Nancy D. O'Reilly, PsyD,** is a bestselling author, educator, philanthropist, and longtime advocate for women's leadership and gender equality. She founded Women Connect4Good, Inc., a 501(c)3 organization committed to empowering women to lead.

Dr. Nancy works closely with those committed to women's advancement and serves on the boards of several national organizations. An in-demand speaker, she has spoken to audiences nationwide, including at the ERA Reception at the U.S. Senate and the Roosevelt House Public Policy Institute at Hunter College in New York.

She also collaborates with her daughter, Ragan Thomson, to lead workshops focused on healing, sacred bonds, and generational transformation.

🌐 www.DrNancyOReilly.com
📷 @drnancyoreilly
Scan QR code to learn more about Dr. Nancy O'Reilly.

# Section IV: Healing, Forgiveness & Legacy

- What am I ready to release, with compassion for myself and others?

- What meaning has emerged from what I have lived through?

- What do I want to carry forward, and what ends with me?

EVERY STORY HOLDS THE POSSIBILITY OF BECOMING SOMETHING NEW.

# 15

# The Alchemy of Forgiveness: Catalyst to Our Souls' Awakening

*by Ragan Thomson*

I was born into light—or at least that's how the memory feels when I allow myself to remember the smallest, truest parts of who I was. There are pictures of me in fluffy dresses, my small "tappy" shoes, as I called them, and a grin that folded itself around the world like a blessing. My first essence was luminosity: a soft yes to life, a tender openness that trusted all. Somewhere along the way, that particular light began to flicker. It did not go out all at once; it was not the sudden snap of a candle smothered by a gust. It dimmed bit by bit: a slow and careful extinguishing shaped by the weather in the house, by the heavy currents that moved through our rooms like climate—pressure, worry, and an undercurrent of thirst and ache that no one could quite name.

I wanted closeness. Who doesn't? I wanted to press into the warmth of the person who birthed me and be held, literally and energetically, with the kind of safety that mends a thousand micro-wounds. But when I turned toward her in those early years, what I felt was a mismatch. Our energies collided more than they met. She moved like someone who had learned to armor her edges, not deliberately against me, but against a life that had asked more of her than she understood she could give. She spoke of choosing me, of seeing my smile at birth, and the sweetness of those confessions hung in the air like a promise. Still, between the testimony of love and the texture of daily living, there was a dissonance.

It is strange and tender to tell the truth: I felt unseen. Not in the grand dramatic sense of being completely invisible, but in the quiet, corrosive way a lack of attunement seeps into a child's bones. She was searching for herself, wrestling with expectations, the edges of her dreams peeled thin by responsibility and the particular humiliation of feeling trapped. There was anger and depression in the house that moved like weather—sometimes a storm, sometimes a heavy fog. There was work, and drinking, and a perfectionism that cut off tenderness. In that climate, the little bright thing that was me reached instinctively for survival. It learned different costumes.

I traded dresses for warm-up suits and the culture of competition. I wore speed, strength, and competence like armor: excellence in sport, sharpness, a certain competitive assurance that got noticed and rewarded in ways softer things didn't. Where once I danced in ribbons, I began to run, to jump, to polish a body into results. I learned to be masculine to be safe. In that acquiring of a tougher edge, I lost parts of my own feminine light—not because it was wrong to play sports or to be strong, but because the shift felt like a sacrifice performed on an altar of belonging. Each time I pushed away my tender inclinations to fit into the household's rhythm, a filament of my original glow went dark.

And yet, even through the distance and the friction, I watched her. I saw in her a similar light, but not the same shape as mine. Hers was pragmatic, flintier; a survivalism that had the nobility of someone trying to hold together the pieces of a life. She was asking questions in a way that sometimes made me feel seen: classes, books, late-night conversations where she tried to seek who she might be beyond the roles she had learned to play. That seeking gave me hope. It meant that perhaps, someday, there would be a meeting. Not the instant, fairy-tale closeness I had desired, but a slow, honest convergence of two people learning to hold themselves.

It took years, decades really, for that convergence to begin. It was not an event but a series of insistences: a seminar we attended together, a conversation opened like a window in a room that had hardly seen air. When we allowed ourselves to speak without the roles we'd been assigned, the truth of our suffering surfaced.

She said things I could hardly hold: words about feeling trapped in pregnancy, about a purpose she could not yet name, about a marriage crowded with expectations and the quiet pressure to be perfect. Her confessions were not excuses. They helped me see the inner world she had been surviving within. The distance I once took personally began to look different. It was not rejection. It was the shadow-work of a woman who had been sacrificing parts of herself just to endure.

I had my own confessions to make. For a long time, I held an internal narrative that painted her as "the one who didn't give enough." It was an understandable story; it made the pain tangible and therefore manageable. But as I turned inward—because healing asks you to do that hard, holy thing of facing yourself—I found a different interior terrain. There were rooms within me where I still felt abandoned, where the little girl who loved glitter and gentle songs curled up and shivered. I had reacted to survival by hardening myself: drugs, alcohol, numbing, affairs—temporary instruments that made the hurt quieter but did not heal it. Against the bright backdrop of the soul, these were only shadows pretending to be shelter.

My path back to light was, paradoxically, inward. It began with small practices that felt almost silly at first: breathing, centering, sitting in a room where there was nothing to do but feel. I called in help—healers, spiritual teachers, circles that taught me to tend to the child within. There was a woman, a teacher, whose work with inner child healing became a compass for me. In the quiet and tender exchanges of therapy and group work, I held the young parts of myself and listened. I learned to name the grief I had swallowed whole and to let it move through me instead of hardening into a story.

And as I worked, I noticed something important: forgiveness began as an inside job. The narrative that I needed her to apologize to me was incomplete. Yes, her apologies came later, and they were meaningful, but the real work was my willingness to forgive myself for having been so small and so hard; to forgive myself for the decisions I made under duress, and for wanting to be loved in a way I could not demand. Forgiveness, in this slow opening, was not an absolution of harm into nothingness; it was a reorientation of my heart. It loosened the tension that had kept me sharp and defensive, slowly allowing tenderness back into my posture.

Once forgiven, I began to see her with different eyes. I started to recognize the contours of her pain and how they had co-shaped mine. When she began to do her own work and learned to ask for forgiveness, not as an end, but as a doorway to forgiving herself, the energy between us shifted. Accountability became our common language. She began to name the ways she had been present and the ways she had been absent. Her humanness, finally articulated, made room for me to grieve and also to rejoice. We did not erase the past. We told it aloud, together, with reverence and sorrow, with a fierce commitment not to repeat the patterns that had nearly undone us.

We went public, oddly and beautifully, as a pair of women who had once been at a distance. We stood together in rooms where other mothers and daughters were also carrying invisible hurts, offering our story as a possible bridge toward reconnection. It felt like a sacrament each time we shared: the admission of difficulty, the articulation of the small mercies, the declaration that healing is not only possible but a practice. People came to us with tears in their eyes; some carried rage, some carried resignation. In offering our wounds and our repair, we discovered the sacredness of being witnesses to another person's return to their center.

Over the last couple of years, the shift became visible. It showed up in her voice, her posture, her laughter. The woman who once traveled in heavy clothes of perfection and pressure now seemed lighter. I could feel her forgiveness as a gift she offered me. I also noticed how this gave relief to her. We began to play. The discovery was almost childish in its simplicity: laughter at the table, unforced conversations, the miracle of small rituals. We began to sit together in spiritual gatherings, to walk into houses of worship side by side, to share silence without the old hunger of needing to be saved by one another. We were whole enough to sit with each other's tender and difficult places and to love them.

There is grief woven into this gratitude. I count our time like one might count the petals of a beloved flower, mindful of the finite gift that is *presence*. Some days, I sit in meditation and call her into the center of my heart, imagining the ribbon of love that always existed between us, however frayed and tangled it had been. In those meditations, I expand the sense of connection until the borders of self dissolve into a warm, unnameable field. I breathe into the knowledge that whether our mothers are walking beside us in flesh or in memory, the work of healing is ours to carry.

To anyone reading this who carries a worn map of maternal distance, know this: there is no linear script to reconciliation. The road is not tidy. It is messy with old stories, random acts of forgetting and remembering, and the unpredictable kindness of two adults deciding, over and over, to try again. The healing I experienced was not the erasure of pain, but the transmutation of it into a deeper capacity for compassion. Forgiveness does not require forgetting; it requires a willingness to stop using our memory as a weapon against our own hearts.

If you are waiting for your mother to heal before you begin your own healing, keep tending to your own interior. The work I did, sitting with the child inside me, learning to love her, confronting my numbing habits, and seeking out teachers, ritual, and community, became the axis on which change turned. I forgave myself before I could fully forgive her. In freeing myself, I made room for her to free herself. In that space, something miraculous happens. Two imperfect beings can see each other fully and still choose tenderness.

Some moments felt almost profound in their simplicity. I remember a day, not long ago, when we sat in the sun and spoke with no intent other than to be present. She laughed at one of my clumsy metaphors, and the sound surprised us both; it had the cadence of newness. In another, she held my hand while we walked into church and did not flinch when I cried. There were times we argued, times old patterns tugged us back into the past, but the pattern of repair holds now. It is a muscle we exercise: we apologize, we listen, we name what is painful; we take responsibility… and we return to love. The repetition of those small choices has become our chosen legacy.

This is not to say I have "unlearned" my protective edges entirely. I am still a woman who knows how to set boundaries and recognize when certain dynamics are unsafe. The healing did not make me naive; it made me more discerning. It also reintroduced me to a soft center I thought I had lost, a center that loves without losing itself, that can be tender and fierce in equal measure. My femininity returned, not as a fragile costume but as a sovereign garment stitched with resilience. I reclaimed my brightness out of a quiet but undeniable desire to live.

In the crucible of my journey, I realized that the challenges I faced with my mother, amidst the longing for her nurturing presence, became the very catalyst for my transformation. As I stood on the brink of motherhood, that flickering flame within me ignited into a fierce determination—a desire to cleanse my spirit and unveil a more profound love for my children. The harder it was to feel triggered with my children, the more aware I became of my own healing journey. I understood that I needed to show up for them consciously awake, patient, loving, and accountable. Every single moment of irritation or frustration with my children became an invitation to explore the unresolved parts of myself. Through this introspective exploration, I began to invite the Divine Mother into my life, allowing her nurturing energy to guide me. In my quest to become the loving, present mother I yearned to be, I discovered the divine presence I had missed in my own upbringing—a blessing that unfolded as I embraced my role with an open heart.

In telling this story, I want to offer you an invitation: take what applies; leave what doesn't. Perhaps you will see echoes of your own life here: the costume changes you made for survival; the ways you learned to distract yourself from yearning; the slow, patient, almost stubborn work of turning inward. Maybe you will be inspired to ask for help. Perhaps you will be moved to speak, to soften, to be curious about the secret weather in the house you grew up in. Maybe you will forgive yourself first, and in that act open a doorway.

Love between a mother and a daughter is not a simple thing. It is a braided current of longing, expectation, mercy, and pain. It can crack and fray. It can also be rewoven with threads of accountability, courage, and ritual. I have learned to count my breaths and to count her presence as a gift—imperfect but sacred. I do not demand perfection. I ask only for honesty, for the willingness to bring light to what has been hidden.

Today, when we sit together, I sometimes close my eyes and imagine the little child I once was, dancing in some forgotten room. I picture the light I was born into, and recognize it glowing again—faint at times, brilliant at others. Another kind of resilience that carries us both forward. We have transformed the gravity between us into something softer and more elastic. We are learning to move in rhythm rather than resistance, to meet each other with awareness, and to stay open when fear would once have closed us.

Please know you are allowed to want closeness, and you are allowed to want to be free of the past. It's okay to grieve the ways you were not "held" and to choose, with fierce intentionality, to hold yourself now. When you do that, the people around you—often, miraculously, your mother—may come with you. And if they do not, your heart can still expand into the sacred work of making peace with what is. There is room enough for both sorrow and joy, and in that space, the light you thought was lost can be found again.

I choose to share how beautiful it is to acknowledge that my mother is also sharing a chapter in this book—a testament to healing and evolution woven together between us. From the trauma of our past, we rise in shared grace, crafting words that intertwine our stories.

This unexpected journey, born from pain, has blossomed into a collaborative dance of wisdom and growth, leading us towards speaking engagements where we can share our experience together and apart. In the sacred process of healing myself, I found the strength to transcend the wounds of the past, and within this journey, the ethereal presence of Mother Mary enveloped me in her peace. She became my divine mother, a symbol of unconditional love and compassion, reminding me that motherhood is not only a relationship but a sacred calling. With her gentle spirit as my compass, I discovered that our shared chapters were not only a reflection of our struggles but also a celebration of transformation—the intertwining of her lessons with the wisdom I have gleaned through my own experiences.

Together, we write not in isolation but in unity, shedding the layers of misunderstanding and embracing a deeper connection that resonates through our shared stories. This is the beauty of our evolution: the recognition that we are co-creators of healing, a dance that reverberates with the sacred echoes of the divine mother. As we step into this new chapter, I am filled with gratitude for the journey that brought us to this moment and for the sacred bonds that forever connect us, illuminating the path for others who seek to heal their own mother-daughter relationships.

Ragan Thomson (right) with her mom, Dr. Nancy O'Reilly

# Ragan Thomson

**Ragan Thomson** is a spiritual teacher, healer, and transformational guide devoted to soul-centered healing and love-led leadership. With more than two decades of experience in spiritual practice and conscious service, her work bridges divine guidance with embodied integration, supporting individuals and groups in reconnecting with their inner truth, resilience, and innate wisdom.

Ragan works intuitively with Spirit, creating safe and reverent containers where breath, presence, and compassionate awareness allow held pain, unconscious patterns, and inherited imprints to be gently witnessed and transformed. Her approach is integrative and grounded, weaving together guided presence, fragmented parts integration, guided forgiveness, gratitude practices, and somatic attunement to support nervous-system regulation and deep internal clearing of mind, body, and spirit, leading to sustainable inner change.

In addition to her intuitive work, Ragan is a Divine I AM practitioner, EFT assist, and certified transformational life coach. She also engages in planetary and collective healing through conscious grid anchoring, supporting harmony and coherence at both personal and global levels. Her work invites a return to sovereignty, clarity, and living from one's divine core.

⊕ www.RaganThomson.com

@ @ragan_thomson

Scan QR code to learn more about Ragan Thomson.

# 16

# The Sacred Thread

*by Sandi Duverneuil*

The bonds between mothers and their children transcend logic. Sometimes the calendar knows before the body does.

## January 15

I woke to damp sheets.

Thirty-two weeks pregnant, I assumed it was one of those late-pregnancy mishaps no one warns you about. I called the after-hours number, trying not to sound worried.

"You're probably fine since you don't feel contractions," the nurse said. "But drive over to the hospital just to be safe."

My then-husband never learned to drive, having grown up in Paris. So I drove forty minutes from suburban Maryland into Washington, DC, unaware that I was in labor. The contractions were there; I just couldn't feel them.

The ER doctors panicked. Shots to stop labor. Immediate admission. Hospital bed rest. I called my mom in Florida and reassured her that the baby and I were both fine. She flew up the next day. At the time, I didn't understand why she seemed so stressed. Was it because this would be her first grandbaby?

Almost a year later, after we moved into my grandmother's aunt and uncle's house, I found an old calendar from 1973, left behind on Aunt Freda's washing machine. My heart suddenly dropped: 1973 was the year my brother died.

I knew Billy drowned after falling through thin ice in Centerport Harbor, but we never observed the anniversary. My younger sister and I weren't allowed to attend his funeral. We had never known the exact date.

I flipped the calendar pages, my eyes landing immediately on the notation: *January 15. Billy died.*

The same day, my water broke.

No wonder my mother had fallen apart.

## First Child: Against All IVF Odds

My journey to motherhood began with a doctor who led me down the wrong path. After my first failed attempt at artificial insemination, my intuition screamed that something was wrong. The doctor's bedside manner was cold. I'd been left alone on a hospital bed after the procedure—no instructions, no timeline, wondering if anyone remembered I existed.

Because my employer was near George Washington Hospital, I got a second opinion at a highly regarded fertility clinic. The specialist didn't mince words. "The ob/gyn should never have wasted your time on artificial insemination. Given your circumstances, IVF is medically necessary. Otherwise, you'd have better luck throwing darts at your uterus."

I'll never forget the phone call from the nurse after my first round of IVF. "Only three embryos to transfer." Her disappointment was unmistakable. At my age, she expected more. "Don't get your hopes up."

I remember thinking: *Right. I'll show you.*

Defying the odds, I became pregnant on our first IVF attempt.

## Second Child: The Odyssey

Trying for a second child made *The Odyssey* sound like a day trip.

After six failed IVF attempts, I was done. No stamina left for fertility cocktails, blood draws, or disappointment. Then my employer announced a reduction in our workforce: our competitor was buying us out. The severance package included six months of employer-paid COBRA insurance.

The clock was ticking.

I remain grateful that my progressive, employee-owned company covered 100% of every IVF attempt. In the clinic's waiting room, I sat beside women who, if they were lucky, had two, maybe three IVF cycles covered before paying tens of thousands out of pocket.

Just as I resigned myself to stopping, my IVF doctor asked an unexpected question.

"Where are you from?"

"New York," I said, confused.

She laughed. "No—I mean your ancestors."

"Latvian, Lithuanian, British, German."

Her face lit up. "With northern European ancestry, there's a high probability you have celiac disease." She asked if I'd be willing to test for celiac antibodies, and if positive, try one last IVF attempt after going gluten-free for a few months.

I tested positive.

This was 2003. No gluten-free aisles, no helpful labels. I ate simply: meat, rice, potatoes, and vegetables. I don't know if eliminating gluten made the difference. But I'm grateful she knew to test.

Here's the cosmic timing part.

Saturday: I was accepted into the Japan Exchange Teaching (JET) program.

Monday: My last IVF attempt was successful.

We'd transferred all five embryos—the clinic's maximum. The doctor couldn't initially tell if I was pregnant with one baby or more based on early bloodwork results.

Sometimes, when you stop forcing an outcome, multiple doors open at once.

I felt light. Relieved. As if I'd been holding my breath for years and could finally exhale. For months, I'd been gripping two impossibilities: becoming a mother again and living my dream of teaching in Japan. The JET acceptance came first—thousands of applicants for a few hundred spots. Then the pregnancy confirmation. My seventh and final IVF attempt, the last one my expiring insurance would cover.

Standing in my kitchen, holding both pieces of news, I understood this wasn't just a coincidence.

I would have gone to Japan regardless. But this was my last chance at IVF—no more insurance, no more IVF attempts. But the universe had other plans. Both doors opened because I finally stopped demanding and started trusting.

## Motherhood Across Cultures: Japan – The Collective Embrace

Becoming a mother in two countries taught me this: children thrive when parents aren't drowning in childcare costs or forced to bootstrap through exhaustion. Japan cared for new mothers; the United States expected them to care for themselves.

In Japan, my c-section recovery included a full week's rest in a private clinic where meals alternated between Western spa cuisine and *kaiseki*—seasonal, artfully presented Japanese haute cuisine. On discharge day, I was offered an aromatherapy massage.

New mothers received a lump-sum payment plus a monthly government allowance—Japan's way of addressing its low birthrate. What struck me is that the money went directly into the mother's bank account.

After six weeks of paid maternity leave, I returned to work. I had a special teaching contract; otherwise, I could have stayed home longer. When our baby was nine months old, and his dad took a part-time teaching job, we needed daycare. Our older son's preschool director helped us get onto the city's public daycare waitlist.

The day the city ward office called with an available spot, we were in the middle of a typhoon.

"Do I really have to come out in this?" I asked.

"Yes," they said. "If you don't come today, the spot goes to the next person."

My mom was visiting. Together, we braved heavy winds and rain—two generations of mothers doing what needed to be done.

## America: The Bootstrap Reality

My U.S. childbirth experience was bleak by comparison.

After two weeks of hospital bed rest, with contractions I couldn't feel and emergency shots to stop labor, my son was born. Initially breech, he turned overnight, canceling the planned c-section. I was induced. The induction failed. His heart rate plummeted. I was rushed into surgery for an emergency C-section.

We were fortunate to be at a hospital equipped for neonatal emergencies.

Two and a half days later, I was discharged. My premature baby remained in the NICU for ten days, confined to an incubator, tethered to wires.

The contrast was unmistakable. In America, new mothers bootstrap. In Japan, they are held.

## Trusting Mother's Intuition

Early in motherhood, I discovered our pediatrician was dismissive. Exhausted from sleepless nights—our baby wouldn't sleep unless pressed against my heart—I was looking for answers.

"It's just colic," he said, waving aside my concern, treating me like a nervous first-time mother.

I'd already learned not to trust careless medical authority after watching my mother question pediatricians who couldn't diagnose my younger sister's childhood illness. I sought a second opinion. The new pediatrician, a woman from New York like me, took one look and diagnosed a double inguinal hernia, common in premature boys, requiring time-sensitive surgery before it became an emergency.

The hernia incident taught me not to let condescension override my intuition.

## Double Vision

Years later, my younger son began crying every morning before school. No explanation.

Bullying? No. Behavior problems? No. Learning delays? No.

His teachers adored him. He struggled with math and organization, nothing alarming. His vision screenings were perfect.

Still, something was wrong.

I mentioned it to my mom. She suggested a developmental optometrist—a specialty I'd never heard of. Insurance didn't cover it, so I paid out of pocket, feeling desperate. The night before the appointment, my son said quietly, "The words from one page keep floating over to the other when I read."

The exam confirmed 20/20 vision. But his visual processing was impaired. Text drifted between pages. Numbers in math columns wouldn't stay in place.

Diagnosis: suppression of binocular vision, convergence insufficiency. His eyes and brain weren't working together.

He began vision therapy several times a week, then twice weekly, for nine months. The treatment emptied my flexible spending account. It was worth every penny. Vision therapy changed his life.

Later, his provider told me that many children with similar symptoms are misdiagnosed with ADHD. My son was lucky—he didn't fidget, so no one labeled him.

I asked my mom how she'd known about developmental optometry. A friend of hers, another New York transplant in Florida, had been diagnosed in her sixties and attended group vision therapy alongside children.

Once again, my mom reminded me that intuition isn't anxiety, it's intelligence. When authority fails, get that second opinion.


**The Sacred Thread**

Motherhood taught me to trust my intuition. Certainty, accepted too early, would have cost me motherhood. Timing can be inexplicable, even cosmic. What are the odds that my final IVF attempt and acceptance into JET would arrive within days of each other?

Humor and defiance are survival tools. In uncertain times, laughter regulates the nervous system.

The bond between mothers and children transcends logic. We know when something's wrong, even before we know why.

## Matrilineal Wisdom

The women in my family have always known things we couldn't explain.

My great-great-grandmother escaped an abusive husband in England by boarding a ship to America. She became a bigamist, not out of recklessness, but survival. Defiance was her inheritance.

My great-grandmother, whose face I share, twins across time, died when my grandmother was nine. Childhood ended that day. Her stepmother rehomed her and her brother. She lived with her high school English teacher and wasn't given the opportunity to attend college, only secretarial school. She never had an advocate.

So my grandmother became a fierce, stubborn Taurus. She treated legal battles like sport, pouring thousands into a real estate case to expose who she believed was a dishonest home inspector. On a brighter note, she and my mom could spot beauty in other people's trash, restore it, and sell it for profit. They made something from nothing.

My mom attended Cornell University before marrying my dad and transferring to Queens College. Education mattered in our family—descendants of Latvian and Lithuanian garment manufacturers and smart, scrappy women who built lives from nothing. My grandmother's half-sister, Judiann Densen-Gerber, earned both an MD and a JD and founded Odyssey House. My grandmother's grandfather, Julius Gerber, served as the executive secretary of New York's Democratic Socialist Party and was portrayed by William Daniels in the 1980s film *Reds*.

We came from fighters.

My mom lost her firstborn, my brother, Billy, in an accidental drowning. The grief sliced a permanent scar in her heart. She became a fierce protector of my sister and me, but never hypervigilant. Mom trusted her intuition above all else.

Once, when I called her an atheist in middle school, she corrected me sharply. "I'm agnostic," she said. "I haven't completely ruled out God." In her heart, I suspect she believed my brother Billy was still watching over us from somewhere beyond the veil.

She was open to astrology, to signs, to trusting the quiet whispers when something wasn't right. When doctors dismissed a giant lump in my sister's neck, my mom sought second opinions until she had answers. In business, she trusted her instincts. When she declined to work with a potential client, she learned a few weeks later that he was arrested in a major drug bust.

Once, returning from Canada, she missed a flight from Toronto to the U.S. That flight crashed.

After that, she believed deeply in divine timing. In delays that save lives. In surrender.

"Don't push," she'd tell me. "If there's a delay, trust it. You may be avoiding a disaster you can't see."

I feel her presence now—in a magnetic pull toward unexpected places, in dreams so vivid they arrive as messages, in a voice that sounds exactly like hers when I face a difficult choice. I call it my Betsy Meyer moxie.

My sons carry the creative and intuitive gifts of this matrilineal line. My grandmother was highly artistic. My mom was a gifted fiber artist, a textile creator, echoing our ancestors in the garment trade, though she never grew up among them.

The thread runs through generations: resilience, creativity, intuition, defiance when authority fails.

This is what I want my sons to know:

Your great-great-grandmother fled violence and crossed an ocean alone. Your great-grandmother died young, but her face lives on in mine. Your grandmother (Mamie) lost a son and learned to trust her intuition.

Mamie taught me to question authority, seek second opinions, and trust what I know.

Standing on the shoulders of these women, I learned to advocate for you. When doctors dismissed the hernia, I sought another opinion. When your eyes and brain couldn't work together, I trusted something was wrong and found the answer, thanks to my mother. When the universe opened two doors at once—Japan and motherhood—I learned to surrender and receive.

Though my mom is no longer here, I know she's watching, proud of her grandsons.

As I move into my next chapter, I ask myself: *What words of wisdom would Mom share with me?*

Her voice still guides me. The sacred thread between mothers and children doesn't break, even beyond the veil. It weaves wisdom, intuition, fierce love, and creative fire through generations.

My younger son graduated cum laude from a Big Ten university—the same child who once couldn't keep text from floating between pages or numbers in columns.

He stands tall.

And now I stand behind him, the way my mother stood behind me, the way her mother wished someone had stood behind her, the way my great-great-grandmother stood alone on a ship headed toward an unknown future.

This is the matrilineal gift: generations of women trusting what they know, defying what doesn't serve them, and passing forward fierce, intuitive love.

Education. Creativity. Resilience. Intuition.

This is our inheritance. This is our legacy.

* * *

**Reflection:** *What has your intuition been trying to tell you that you've been too afraid, or too busy, to hear?*

Sandi Duverneuil and her mom Betsy Meyer

# Sandi Duverneuil

**Sandi Duverneuil** is a poet, writer, and mother of two who has spent much of her life navigating thresholds—between cultures, languages, and versions of herself.

She has lived and worked across the United States, Canada, Japan, and France, each experience deepening her understanding of what it means to adapt, belong, and find voice amid constant change. Her journey through infertility, motherhood, expatriate life, and maternal loss has shaped her perspective on resilience, identity, and the quiet wisdom passed through the maternal line.

Through *Peonies & Prose*, Sandi creates poetry, prose, and art for those navigating life's thresholds—offering language as a companion for grief, reawakening, and reclaiming creative life. She also offers private poetic transmissions, pairing intuitive writing with original artwork for those seeking reflection during pivotal moments.

Her Substack serves as a gathering place for thoughtful reflection on creativity, identity, and navigating life's transformations.

⊕ www.PeoniesAndProse.com

⊙ @peonies_prose

Scan QR code to learn more about Sandi Duverneuil.

# 17

# A River Wave of Light

*by Ellie Epstein-White*

Our song sings through me like a love letter to you, Mom. I remember making a mixed CD for you, including a more contemporary song we both liked: *Truly, Madly, Deeply* by Savage Garden. I never realized how this song would unite us over the years. I have stood with you both on mountain tops and bathed with you in bodies of water. Here I am releasing this story into the arms of Mother Earth like a river wave of light.

I was wading in ocean deep grief, while also celebrating a beautiful July day, walking where the water met the shoreline along Wells Beach in Maine, one of your favorite beaches. The sand, small stones, shells, and water washed against my ankles and feet like a massage. I remember loving the sounds of the ocean: the waves beating the shoreline like a sacred drum. The birds were making their own music, singing an ethereal tune. The duality of the water, warm one moment and cold the next, creating a feeling of finding balance in holding space. Feathers swimming with grace in the ocean, perhaps signaling that angels were near. You were not physically there, but I felt your presence, your soft blanket of love.

It was at this spot that I received a download, a channeled poem that helped me understand grief with a whole new perspective. It was almost like the message was whispered in the wind. I saw the sun on the horizon, glowing brilliantly like golden honey. The sky was deep, breathing blue, scattered with clouds. All of a sudden, the beautiful blue sky wept violet, becoming darker, a midnight indigo bursting with storm clouds. I had made it safely back to the car before a concert of rain fell from the sky. After the storm, a rainbow smiled, gracing the sky with beauty after the storm. In the car, I transcribed the words I received from the beach into my phone. And I polished it into the following poem:

In the storm you face,
A deep, dark blue curtain of clouds looms overhead,
Dumping a waterfall of tears from the Sky.
I am the Rainbow, sparkling,
Where Sun meets Rain.
I smile upon you,
Watching and guiding you on.
Know in the jewel of your heart that I am not lost.
I took over the world in arcs of color,
wrapping and surrounding you
in all my love.
I will not fade out.
I can be found sitting on top of the world,
Dreaming of what was, what is, and what is to come.
I'll be painting the world in all my colors, watching everything from
Above, paying tribute to you and all my animal friends.
I am on an adventure, taking flight with the birds,
forever chasing Stars in the Milky Way.
Now is the time, I must leave you, and hand over my torch to you.
May you find comfort in the memories we quilted together,
And peace with every breath I was to take.
Remember, I'll light up your darkest hour with the sound of smiles
and drum up life into
every heartbeat.
I'll be your anchor through storms.
In every step you walk, may you find solace in knowing that I am
still with you.
With all my love shining upon you, I found a place to live deep
within your heart.

These words I wrote down helped me begin to see grief as another facet of love; love being transformed into a new state. Writing helped me translate my feelings of grief and pain into language and language into connections. In writing, I learned what you already knew: I used "writing to work out my problems." Mom, you felt that I was surely going to be a writer, and you would never have dared hope for this before it actually happened. You felt I was carrying on your dearest ambitions.

Just as Gloria Steinem, you, Mom, felt the weight and calling of living "the unlived life of your mother." I, in turn, sense that I have lived your unlived life. The women in our family mapped the terrain before me—clearing brush, laying stone, widening and paving the path. What distinguishes their lives from mine was chiefly a matter of time and place: an unfolding arc of history in which the boundaries of womanhood stretched beyond their former confines, and the rights and privileges of citizenship came to be more fully realized and honored.

I remember the day I lost you, Mom, like it was a tattoo. It was April 17th, 2014, and I woke up into a living nightmare, staring into a bright blue wall of calm ocean. I heard the phone ringing like a church bell. I already knew who was on the line and the words that would be spoken. Instinctively, I also knew it was the call no one ever wanted to make. I gulped a breath of fresh air and heard a deafening silence. It was the hospital on the line with my father, informing the family of what I intuitively knew all along: You wouldn't recover from your stroke.

The medical team explained that your heart gave out while they were removing your breathing tube. You panicked during the procedure. Due to all your medical ailments—diabetes, cancer, high blood pressure—your heart couldn't withstand the stress… and failed. So, your death was due to complications of a stroke.

All along, the doctors tried to instill hope that you would survive your stroke, but they couldn't say what conditions you would face if you recovered. The family had attended a local Jewish Film Festival at the Red River Theater in Concord when your stroke unexpectedly arrived. Your face drooped like a half moon, and you held a Mona Lisa smile, drooling part of your last meal of popcorn. An ambulance was called. You were extricated from the movie theater and rushed to the Concord Hospital.

April 2014 arrived like a mixed bag of weather. Spring was here, and soon the blooms of daffodils and tulips would sprout through the lips of the earth, and pansies would shine their beautiful heads in the sunlight. It was Passover, and this year we canceled our Seder because of your condition. I felt this year that our house was marked, and we were not passed over.

If you were unable to care for yourself and move on your own, you would have soon made your peace and released yourself from your body. Regardless, Mom, you were no longer with us. It took you eleven whole days before you decided to make your exit from the human world. Over time, I would learn to feel your presence in my heart and feel you in spirit. I already felt like you rode along in the car with us, as Dad and I made an emergency trip to the hospital, an hour-long commute. Still, I felt hollow like a carved-out Pumpkin, celebrating Halloween.

Like a creation myth, Mom, you became part of the stars; a constellation in my sky. Mom, you were the Sun in my solar system, smiling and watching over me. I felt your magic embrace me, envelope me like a warm, soft, gentle blanket. A cold chill charged through my body, but I felt warmth shine like golden diamond nuggets of sun.

At the hospital, I felt like I was tuned to automatic autopilot. Everything at the hospital was a blur. I remember feeling your cold body. In my moment of grief, I needed to take pictures of your dead body. This might be construed as morbid, but I needed pictures as evidence, proof that you were no longer with us. Maybe I would "capture your soul" in my photo shoot, as some cultures believe. I wanted pictures honoring your final resting place, so I could remember that you did not just disappear and go traveling on a long vacation, only to return home one day in the future. I was not ready to say goodbye. One of the ICU nurses tried to comfort me, telling me she could tell Mom, you loved me, because she could see Celia Thaxter's "sunset's dying smile" of love within your eyes.

As Dad and I sat in the office at the funeral home, I felt grief burning me up like a raging forest fire. We were there to discuss funeral arrangements. Dad and I picked out a beautiful urn, one with a beautiful mosaic of purple and blue butterflies. Together, Dad and I planned a beautiful ceremony for you, Mom; so many people attended. What I remember most about your celebration of life ceremony was not being able to give a eulogy and pick out the perfect words to speak and commemorate you. Ever since, I have been looking for the perfect piece of writing to honor you.

At the time, I felt like a sturdy, steady tree—standing strong for my family, carrying on in the slow pulse of life. Yet the irony was that I clung so tightly to the rope of life that I stumbled along in oblivion, barely breathing. Years later, I was encouraged to try yoga. From there, I embraced the yogic journey, diving deep into my own soul. I began a personal self-study, slowly unraveling layers of hurt and pain, peeling back the wounds life had handed me. Gradually, I gathered tools for my inner toolbox—creating a garden within and planting seeds meant to grow and take root. After your death, I needed to rebuild my foundation, carefully selecting the ingredients for the life I was now being asked to live. Still, I remained blind to the truth that growth, like the plants in a garden, comes with its own growing pains. One of my teachers once told me that the most powerful form of yoga is the "yoga of relationships," where everyday interactions with partners, family, and friends become tools for living life fully. When you realize that "it's all yoga," you begin to meet people where they are, stretching the pose of your own heart to find ease and comfort in the places where you meet each other. This, I've learned, is far more transformational and profound than any asana on the mat. It is the slow unrooting of old ways of bracing, and the brave, daily practice of bending without breaking.

After the loss of you, Mom, I felt like I was perpetually underwater, weighted down by stones, as if slowly drowning, gasping for air. Yet you kept tapping my shoulder, whispering, "Time to wake up now. Turn your lead into gold. Be the Philosopher's Stone." Gradually, I softened into your new way of being, learning to rest in the quiet comfort of your transformation and making space for your presence in spirit. Though your body was gone, you lived within my heart— guiding my writing, meeting me in meditation, and breathing love into what had once felt like absence.

I remember a conversation you and I had while you were writing a biography on the Beecher Sisters. You discussed Spiritualism and the idea that Isabella Beecher Hooker did not want to say goodbye to her mother. Isabella, a Spiritualist, believed the veil separating the living and the dead was thin and that the living and the dead could correspond. Like you, Mom, Isabella also suffered from a stroke in January of 1907, lingering a few days before passing. She was among the many in the women's movement whose legacy of establishing voting rights for women went unfinished. Isabella patiently worked with great leaders of the Women's movement, Lucretia Mott, Elizabeth Cady Stanton, and Susan B. Anthony—women you idolized and to whom the civilized world owes an immeasurable debt of gratitude. Like many foremothers of the women's movement, you were mindful and careful of public perception.

Mom, you loved cats. I got a kick out of how you named your feline friends after women from history. You named the first cat I ever knew, T.C., after Tennessee Claflin. T.C. did not stand for "The Cat." T.C. tried on my nightgowns and shared my crib. She loved being outside. She would meow at the sliding door when it was cold and rainy—not to come inside, but to complain that we hadn't turned off the rain. We lost T.C. the night of your retirement party from the university. She was waiting for us when we came home, barely able to move, struggling to reach her food and water bowls. I knew immediately that something was wrong. By the end of the night, she was wrapped in your newly acquired scarf, ready to be laid to rest. T.C. succumbed to kidney disease. Celebration and grief arrived in the same breath, teaching me early how joy and loss can share the same doorway.

In the next chapter of cats, we welcomed Harriet and Isabella. They entered our lives around the time I left for college, to keep you company while I was away. The siblings—a brother and sister—were named after the Beecher sisters, Harriet Beecher Stowe and Isabella Beecher Hooker, the subjects of the book you were researching in 2000. They were dueling siblings, each vying for our attention. Both crossed the animal rainbow bridge just before you had your stroke.

Like Isabella Beecher Hooker, you were a modern-day woman. Mom, you wanted to have it all—and struggled with the question so many women before and after you have faced: *How much of myself should I give to being a good wife and a good mother?* You wanted to plan your career, figure out when to marry and have children, and avoid conflicts experienced by women. You did not want to walk the traditional path, trying to break free of the confines of women's roles and the labels and boxes society places us in.

When you were a teenager, you were one of the many who became pregnant by their high school boyfriends. Mom, you turned to your mother, a professional nurse, to help provide resources and arrange medical care with all her connections, supporting you to hide and terminate your pregnancy. In this way, Mom, you avoided the traditional path for a woman: being trapped in the common sense of marriage by pregnancy. Both you and your mother traveled far from home to see a doctor who would induce a miscarriage under risky conditions. This action liberated you, Mom, buying you a "get out of jail" card, leasing you a fresh set of new opportunities, so you could lead your best life. You excelled in school and were provided an opportunity to attend college and graduate school, eventually obtaining your PhD.

Mom, you valued the importance of a good education and devoted your professional life to teaching Women's Studies at the University of New Hampshire. On some level, you viewed your work as a teacher as "saving the world… one student at a time," looking to educate minds and enrich lives. However, Mom, you became so bogged down with the politics of the university, it soon drained your energy and gave your body aches from toe to crown. At night, you listened to relaxation and meditation to wind down from the chaos of life. Still, you were plagued by extreme cases of insomnia, feeling too keyed up, and wound up like a Yo-Yo by everything to sleep properly. Over time, you realized your insomnia might be caused by the "meetings" you were involved with at the university.

Even in the Women's Studies department at UNH, you felt a resistance to your stance on politics and women's issues. Mom, you learned to choose your battles, realizing you needed to speak out when it mattered, even when it was considered unpopular. But you still felt there were times when you should have kept your mouth shut, despite the voice in your head insisting that your colleagues needed to hear what you had to say. Ultimately, you wanted to feel like you managed to win friends and influence people, yet felt you were gaining more enemies than friends at the university.

Mom, you had an idea to create a course on mothers and daughters in history. You felt it would be a lot of work to design a new course, even if you came up with a course description. When you were grading the "mother biography" papers, you felt it wasn't a good assignment. The students loved writing the papers, but you felt they all had a similar theme:

- My mom and I are best friends.
- She grew up wanting to help people.
- She wanted to become a teacher or a nurse.
- She stayed home after I was born, now works at a (low-paid) job, and is proud to contribute to the family income.

The theme was that life is "perfect" and that the "majority" of moms don't regret a thing.

As you told your students during one of your classes, history doesn't progress in a straight line. One of your classes was on birth control, which you felt was great for a history lesson. Your students read Margaret Sanger's autobiography. In discussion, someone would often remark that it was too bad the nineteenth-century women didn't have birth control.

You wrote on the board the many forms they did have, and then the students had to realize the silencing that had taken place in order for Sanger, a nurse, to have no information about birth control and have to go to Europe to get it. So, the students learnt that everything had a history, even birth control; that it was not progressive, that every right we have as women was won for us by other women and men.

Mom, you lived with a troubling thought: wondering back in the mid-1990s, with the political climate back then, whether the few gains made in the Women's movement would be wiped out completely.

You valued your precious moments of alone time. You longed for entire days alone, so you could work on your writing. You always loved Virginia Woolf's comment that entire days alone were like "pure and rounded pearls." Often, when you thought you had a pearl of an hour alone, the phone would interrupt, reminding you, "O, life's not like that!" The phone call cost you time, eating up most of the pearl of an hour.

By the time you reached your mid-fifties, you were plagued by health problems and stress at the university, leaving you sick at heart and sick in body. You reported that you were "sick of being sick." On more than one occasion, you literally lived the dream of having your tooth fall out at the most inopportune times—when you were about ready to leave for a vacation, when you were in the middle of a meal, or when the dentist was closed over the holidays. It felt like you were always making a trip to the dentist a little too regularly, having scheduled emergency trips for dental procedures, such as replacing a crown, which only led to even more medical problems due to your diabetes.

There were days when you couldn't use your hands because they were plagued by intense pain. Mom, you were unable to write or garden. Every year, you planted your traditional annual pansies, so when Spring arrived, I helped you with this ritual. Pansies were your all-time favorite flowers. You carried fond memories of them from your childhood. You were a wonderful storyteller, and I listened in awe, eating up every word as you told me how pansies were edible—and how you had once eaten them in fancy salads.

No matter how much you tried to conceal your health problems, I could sense the rhythm of your days—frequent trips to the doctor, tireless searches for answers to explain your pain. I remember you voicing your frustration when some doctors dismissed your suffering as psychological—"all in her head." I carried a quiet ache, watching you navigate this labyrinth of care, like an old tree bending with the wind, its roots deep and unshaken despite the storm.

For years, Mom, you played the numbers game with your diabetes, hoping that diet and pills alone could keep it at bay. You explored alternative approaches—from acupuncture to any suggestion you could find—before eventually accepting insulin, a turning point that eased much of the neurological pain you had endured. Over time, we discovered the true source of your suffering: neuropathy, the hidden current beneath the nerve pain that had haunted you for so long. I came to understand that your body was an instrument with a voice of its own, resonating most clearly when you were fully in alignment with yourself.

Through it all, Mom, you were my Superwoman—a radiant blaze of light that dazzled the world like the sun, yet tenderly blanketing me in warmth, like crystalline snow settling softly on the earth. You were the "little train that could," wearing all kinds of hats while striving to break free from living as if you were trapped inside *A Doll's House* by Henrik Ibsen. Mom, you refused to be a stay-at-home wife or mother, suffocating beneath the quiet death of household drudgery. You demanded a public life filled with meaningful work and intellectual engagement, unwilling to accept a society that denied women recognition for having minds of their own—or the right to use them fully. You walked a delicate line, tiptoeing along the tightrope between motherhood and blazing your own path as a professor, leader, and a woman unapologetically yourself.

Regardless of your poor health, you gifted me with a variety of experiences to fill my childhood: travel, family vacations to visit my grandparents, cultural and political events at the university, plays, and concerts. One of my favorite experiences as a child was listening to your stories, especially from when you were younger. These stories were always better than a television program or movie. They sparked me into life, lighting me up like fireworks, strumming a musical chord in me.

One story that plays in my mind around the holidays was the tradition of making "alibi pies" the night before Thanksgiving. As the story was told, both you and my father were interrogated by the police regarding the murder of your former boyfriend, who had been stalking you. Both of you gave your alibi for the night in question: you were both making pies for Thanksgiving. From what you told me about the investigation, you were both ruled out as suspects by forensic science. According to you, Mom, the murder remained unsolved, and the murderer was never found.

What brings me joy is remembering how much you loved to celebrate the holidays: the dazzling bright lights, the food, the music, the company of others. Mom, you brewed love into the food cooked for these occasions and enjoyed the gifts the holidays brought. During these festivities, you felt joyous energy run through the veins of life, bringing the singing bowl of your body ringing into your signature vibration.

Every year, I honored you by reading one of our favorite children's stories, *The Mother's Day Mice* by Eve Bunting to celebrate Mother's Day. The story was about three sibling mice who brave the world to find gifts for their mother. All the mice, but the youngest, find a beautiful, natural gift from the physical world. The youngest mouse finds the perfect gift: a song written from the heart.

If you slept and dreamed, you often recorded it in your journal. One dream lingered in my mind, as if it revealed the heartbeat of our relationship and the delicate balance of family life. We were in Madison, Wisconsin, somehow separated from Dad, who had the car. Mom, you rode a bike, and I clung to the handlebars. Darkness unfolded around us, the streets twisting like rivers with unfamiliar names, and we were lost. You stopped to ask for directions in a warm, well-lit, bar-like place, perhaps off E. Johnson Street. You became absorbed in conversation, relaxed into the glow of human warmth, and eventually found a pay phone to call Dad, who gave you directions. Then, suddenly, you remembered I was outside, waiting. Panic surged through you. It was dark and raining; I was shivering, sick, and fragile, and you feared I might catch pneumonia and die in the night. Too weak to hold on any longer, I sagged against the bike. Mom, you cradled me with one arm while steering with the other. You felt a deep, almost unbearable guilt for having forgotten me, even for a heartbeat. Taken literally, this dream would likely alarm child protective services. Yet I found it fascinating—its intensity, its emotional truth, and the way it captured the fragile, fierce, human dance of care, love, and fear that shaped our bond.

During most of my middle and high school years, I felt lost in a void, falling down the rabbit hole of schoolwork. I was blinded to everything that wasn't homework—to the point of not participating in after-school activities, even with your encouragement. You felt it wasn't necessary for me to live under so much pressure. Mom, you wondered how you could help me realize that I was okay "just the way I was." I was always jammed with papers, projects, or tests. Many long weekends were spent hunched over schoolwork—like sewing a Canadian flag from cloth and stitching it together by hand, or writing and illustrating a short storybook about jaguars. I would spend entire weekends with you, Mom, working side by side on these projects. During my school years, my extracurricular world narrowed to learning the flute and swimming on the team.

I was an avid swimmer, drawn to everything about the water. Once I braved the cold water, my body quickly warmed, burning with a surge of energy after a good workout. I loved the feel of the pool against my skin, the way my breath and stroke moved together in a rhythm that belonged only to me. Looking back, swimming was my aquatic yoga—an arena where I learned focus, patience, and the quiet power of persistence.

During one swim meet, you grew upset when you saw me warming up. I took a few strokes, then instinctively reached back to adjust my straps. You noticed that every other girl's suit had extra support in the back—a detail we hadn't considered when buying mine. True to form, you felt I had neglected to mention the issue beforehand—especially since I'd noticed the problem during practice the week before. When I was young, I didn't always have the language to express my needs, and you carried the quiet anxiety of trying to protect me.

True to your nature, you improvised. Cleverly channeling your inner MacGyver, you borrowed a jackknife from a friend, disappeared into a janitor's closet, and returned with a string you had cut off from a mop. With careful hands and a quiet determination, you tied my bathing suit straps together in the back. Of course, I was worried about how it looked, but your solution carried me through the meet. Afterwards, we went shopping for a proper bathing suit for the swim team. Later, Mom, you questioned your parenting, thinking: *What worse feeling than to realize that you've failed to supply your child with the proper equipment?*

When I told you I planned to continue on the swim team the following year, you gently nudged me toward track instead. You believed I had a gift and excelled at running the mile, trusting the praise of my P.E. teachers. Still, I held my ground—I had chosen swimming as my path. So you supported me, meeting me where I was. To honor my choice, you encouraged me to attend Harvard Swim Camp the first week of July, hoping it would strengthen not only my skills in the water but also help me grow into myself with more confidence.

Looking back, swimming was never just about races or strokes; it was a mirror of life itself—learning to adjust when the unexpected arises, to trust in my own rhythm, and to recognize the quiet, unwavering support of those who love you. In every lap, I felt the lessons of persistence, the pulse of patience, and the certainty that even when the current shifts, I could still find my way.

Mom, you also loved to swim, whether in the pool or at the beach. In the summer, we often visited the Durham Outdoor Pool, where we could swim, and you could attend your aquasize class. The pool was sectioned off and named after various aquatic animals, and it was unique for having a man-made beach area.

One summer afternoon, we were at the pool, and Mom, you felt I had "disgraced myself." Some girls from school wandered over to Whale. I didn't realize it at the time, but I had made the mistake of letting you believe these girls were my "friends." I was at an awkward stage in life—shy and quiet—and had trouble saying a simple "hello," let alone acknowledging them.

Mom, you encouraged me to jump in and play Marco Polo with the girls, but I was uninterested in playing the game—or being social at all—so I just sat on the edge of the pool. During the entire interaction, you felt I acted and looked foolish.

Finally, one of the girls came over and invited me to play. Eventually, I slipped into the water and hovered near the edge, keeping my distance from the group, not really playing the game. When the group moved to Shark, I tagged along but mostly stood on the sidelines.

After the encounter, I could feel your embarrassment radiating toward me. The way I lingered at the edges made you worry people would think I couldn't swim at all. You also read my silence as proof of how socially awkward I was—as if it would be a wonder if I had any friends at all.

Fortunately, you became absorbed in your aquasize class and only climbed out of the water a couple of times to urge me to participate. Even so, you could empathize because you saw me as a mirror of yourself. Somewhere beneath your frustration was a quieter question: *why does she have to be so much like me?* As I grew older, you began to recognize parts of yourself in me. When I was young, you thought I was entirely like my father and hoped I would inherit his love for math. But I was more like you, my heart always leaning toward writing.

One summer, our family went hiking with friends in the White Mountains of New Hampshire. We climbed Mount Doublehead, making it to the summit to enjoy the view from the top. On the way back down the mountain, we were unable to locate the trail. So we had a trusting conversation with the land, and lost ourselves in a forest of trees. We were bushwhacking and stumbling, losing ourselves in brush and bramble, into roots that tested your footing, stumps that slowed you down, and branches that asked you to duck and weave. We were called to listen more closely, wander in patience, and improvise—to each other, to the forest, to the quiet voice that says, *we'll find our way.* We made our path by walking it. We learned that sometimes the way down isn't clear—but it is possible. Eventually, we emerged from the mountain—scratched, tired, and relieved. When we reached the bottom, we renamed the trail: the "happy happy fun trail."

One of our favorite winter activities was sledding. In the deep of winter, you would take my friend, her siblings, their dog, Buffy, and me sledding across the street from our house. We all bundled up in warm winter layers: winter coats, snow pants, gloves, boots, scarves. We trudged through the snow into the woods towards our small hill. The world was hushed and white, a winter wonderland waiting for motion. The snow covered the landscape like a mural of soft kindness, showing us a balance of beauty in a harsh world. You made your way down first, carving the sledding path, showing us the way.

We flew down the hill on fresh snow with Buffy on our ankles, laughing as gravity claimed us, free-falling into joy. Then we climbed back up—again and again—until the cold seeped through our layers and the adrenaline gave way to hunger. We returned home flushed and breathless, shedding winter at the door. In the warmth of the house, we welcomed steaming bowls of ramen noodle soup and mugs of hot cocoa. Warmth returned to our fingers, and life gathered itself back into us.

All these years later, I remain in awe of you, Mom—how you still guide me, still teach me. One afternoon, while working at home, my eyes fell upon a wall hanging you had placed long ago. Bold letters read: "America's Most Dangerous Woman"—J. Edgar Hoover. I had seen it countless times, yet that day, the words spoke with new clarity, like a secret message only I was ready to hear.

This message came to me through Emma Goldman's words, echoing the wisdom of the energy and healing arts that have shaped my own path. In her 1911 essay *The Tragedy of Woman's Emancipation*, she wrote that while the right to vote and equal civil rights may be "good demands," true emancipation begins in a woman's soul. "History shows us," Goldman argued, "that every oppressed class has gained true liberation not through permission granted by its masters, but through its

own efforts. True freedom reaches only as far as our power to claim it."
For Goldman, "inner regeneration" was essential—the cutting of cords
bound by "prejudice, tradition, and custom." Liberation, she reminded
us, could not be achieved at the polls, in courts, or through laws, politics, and institutions alone. The foundation for a "clean slate" had to be
laid elsewhere—untainted and deeply rooted within. It was a reminder
that the most radical revolution is always inward—and that liberation,
love, and power begin in the quiet, luminous spaces within.

I felt this truth resonate through me as I recalled a channeled poem I
had received on the beach. Its words had flowed like jewels of love,
blanketing me in the highest power. I could feel the mantra, *Aham
Prema*, vibrating through every cell:

*"You'll be my anchor through storms. In every step I walk, may I find
solace in knowing that you are still with me. With all your love shining
upon me, you found a place to live deep within my heart."*

Ellie Epstein-White and Mom

# Ellie Epstein-White

**Ellie Epstein-White** is a best-selling author featured in the *Life Changing Energy* anthologies—*The Call Within: Finding Purpose and Sparking Transformation* and *Whispers of the Soul: Stories of Resilience, Awakening, and the Power of Healing Within*—as well as the *Awakened Hearts* series, Volumes 1 and 2, and *Hear Us Roar: Black Panther*. A writer at heart and devoted sound and energy practitioner, Ellie has a unique ability to alchemize words, vibration, and ritual into sacred portals of healing, self-discovery, and embodied empowerment.

She feels a deep sense of purpose in sharing her writing as a way of healing herself while inspiring others to embark on their own Hero's Journey—reclaiming joy, intuition, and inner truth. An avid yoga and meditation practitioner with a profound love for sound, Ellie weaves these practices into both her personal life and creative work.

Professionally, she is employed by the New Hampshire Department of Safety. She is also a member of the Good Energy Healing Club, facilitated by local author and natural health intuitive Hilary Crowley. Through her participation in a wide range of healing arts programs, Ellie holds certifications in Reiki and Sound Healing. She studied minerals and rocks, as well as Usui Reiki Ryoho, with author, teacher, and crystal expert Nicholas Pearson.

Ellie cherishes time with her cat, Robin, along with family and friends. She hopes to guide those who enter her "field of light" toward the practice of *off-the-mat yoga*, using her writing and this chapter as a spark for new beginnings—for herself and others walking the path of awakening.

Ⓕ www.facebook.com/ellie.epstein.white
Scan QR code to learn more about Ellie Epstein-White.

**Hello friend,**

If you've made it here, you've just walked through something meaningful.

Maybe parts of these stories felt familiar. Maybe they stirred something you hadn't looked at in a while. Or maybe they simply reminded you of the depth and complexity of love.

The relationship between a mother and a child is never just one thing. It can be beautiful and challenging, steady and uncertain, healing and unfinished… sometimes all at once.

And yet, it shapes us.

Not just in how we were loved, but in how we learn to love. Not just in what we received, but in what we choose to carry forward.

These stories were never meant to give you answers. They were meant to offer reflection. To remind you that whatever your experience has been, it matters.

So I'll leave you with this…

What feels ready to be softened?
What can be seen with new understanding?
What do you want to carry forward?
You don't have to have it all figured out. Just stay open.

And if something in these pages stayed with you, trust that.

You are not alone.
And love is still unfolding.

David Trotter
Curator / Publisher – *Awakened Hearts*
Co-founder / Publisher – *Awakened Magazine*

*P.S., Will you help us spread these stories of awakening around the globe? Simply post a heartfelt review on Amazon and tell a friend about the book. It's that easy!*

# David Trotter

David Trotter is the curator and publisher of the *Awakened Hearts* book series, a collection of transformational anthologies featuring stories of spiritual awakening, healing, and personal growth. He is also the co-founder and publisher of *Awakened Magazine* (alongside his partner Mandy Adams), and the creator of *Awakened Lifestyle*, an online directory connecting conscious leaders, healers, and coaches with seekers around the world.

David is the author of a dozen books – including *Empowered to Rise* and *Superconscious Conversations* – and the producer/director of four award-winning feature films on meaningful social issues including orphans in India, trafficking in the United States, and LGBTQ inclusion within faith-based communities.

Earlier in his journey, David spent over a decade as a pastor before stepping beyond traditional ministry to embrace a more expansive spiritual path. He holds a B.A. in Pastoral Ministries and an M.A. (abt) in Church Leadership from Vanguard University, along with an M.A. in Cross-Cultural Studies from Fuller Theological Seminary.

He is also a Certified Breathwork and Guided Meditation Facilitator and regularly leads sessions at Behind the Lids Healing Collective in Costa Mesa, California.

⊕ www.awakenedmagazine.com
◎ @awakenedmagazine
Scan QR code to learn more about Awakened Magazine.

# Awakened Hearts
# Volume #1

If this book stirred your soul, you must read our first book!
*Awakened Hearts #1* features an inspiring collection of real-life
stories from 32 conscious leaders, healers, spiritual teachers,
and everyday seekers who have experienced profound spiritual
awakening, emotional healing, and personal transformation.

**More information:** www.awakenedmagazine.com/awakenedheartsone

# Awakened Hearts
# Volume #2

*Awakened Hearts #2* is a transformative collection of true stories from 25 conscious leaders, healers, and seekers who have faced the darkness within—and discovered freedom on the other side. Each author's journey reveals a sacred moment of breaking open where pain became power, fear gave way to faith, and truth led to radiant self-expression.

**More information:** www.awakenedmagazine.com/awakenedheartstwo

# awakened
## magazine

**Awakened Magazine** is a leading resource for soulful storytelling, conscious living, and transformative wisdom from today's most inspiring healers, coaches, and spiritual leaders.

Subscribe for free:
www.awakenedmagazine.com

**Awakened Lifestyle** is your go-to directory to discover conscious events, healers, and podcast opportunities – locally and globally.

Explore listings or add your own:
www.awakened.lifestyle

**Awakened Hearts** is a series of heart-opening anthology books featuring real stories of spiritual awakening, healing, and transformation.

Share your story:
www.awakenedheartsbook.com

*We're here to support you on your awakening journey!*